WRITE AND REVEAL

PAULA FRIEDENHAIN

Write and Reveal

INTERPRETATION OF HANDWRITING

PETER OWEN · LONDON

ISBN 0 7206 0102 9

PETER OWEN LIMITED
12 Kendrick Mews Kendrick Place London SW7

Reprinted 1973
First British Commonwealth edition 1959
© Paula Friedenhain 1959

Printed in Great Britain by
Redwood Press Ltd Trowbridge Wiltshire

CONTENTS

ACKNOWLEDGMENTS

Thanks are due to Messrs Allen & Unwin for permission to quote from *Experiments with Handwriting* (1928) and *The Psychology of Handwriting* (1925) by Robert Saudek; to Orell Fussli Verlag for permission to quote from *Symbolik der Handschrift*) by Max Pulver (1931); and to Mrs Ina Dean Farley for her invaluable help to the author in compiling this book, and for her most useful suggestions.

INTRODUCTION

In a sense it is true to say that there is no such thing as 'handwriting' for it is not the hand but the brain which directs our action during the process of writing. The brain transmits impulses through the spinal cord to our arms and hands, so that the wrists, hands and fingers are merely the instruments in use.

Every writing movement consists of an automatic process of expansion and contraction of the muscles which are controlled by the motor nervous system. Writing is therefore an expressive movement and its study is that of a dynamic element.

Whatever characteristics we have, they are likely to be shown in our writing, revealing to a certain extent our true self. We know that conscious processes are mirrored in our writing but we do not realize how much of our hidden self is betrayed by it. It is, in fact, a reflection of our attitude towards self, sex and society.

Just as our way of walking, talking and laughing, our handshake and our general approach to our fellow-beings are an expression of our personality, so handwriting too is a form of selfexpression. But when we write we deem ourselves unobserved. We do not think of the possibility of skilled scrutiny and so we reveal ourselves intimately to the analyst.

Abilities, tendencies, virtues and vices, the general mentality of a writer and his likely reactions to a given situation can all be ascertained by means of a handwriting analysis. Not only can the more obvious things like maturity and manual dexterity be seen in a handwriting but also the 'bent' and gifts of a person, his whims and fancies, his rigidity or adaptability and his social, a-social or anti-social behaviour. His sincerity or attempts at deception are also revealed and no mask, however ingeniously worn, can deceive the graphologist. Chronic and acute illnesses and other special conditions also leave their traces in a script.

Slips of the pen sometimes occur and they are as revealing as slips of the tongue. The cook, for example, whom in answer to an advertisement stated that she was 'an experienced crook' was giving a clear warning to her potential employer. Similarly the traveller who in applying for a post said that he was 'of Scotch rationality' could fairly be suspected of stressing a quality that he feared was lacking in his character.

Industrial, medical and academic psychologists and also child guidance and marriage guidance specialists could all with advantage use the work of the graphologist. The subject of the graphologist's test is unaware of being tested and therefore completely at his ease, whereas the element of anxiety or fear tends to affect the more obvious experiments of other investigators.

The scope of graphology has limitations which no good graphologist overlooks. Graphology is a science that is still in the pioneer stage and therefore humility in the face of many unsolved problems is essential. The more clearly this is stated at the outset the more surely will disappointments be prevented. As we know graphology today it is a comparatively young science with a history of not more than eighty years. However, when it is applied by well-trained writing analysts it can play an important part as a subsidiary to psychology.

There are some things that handwriting cannot tell us. Sex and age cannot be determined from a specimen of handwriting for example. Many men are peculiarly feminine and many women delight in stressing their masculinity by expressing it in their writing. Similarly some people show infantile traits even at a mature age, while others show ataxia and tremor when comparatively young. The graphologist will therefore always have to be furnished with the sex and age of the writer. It would perhaps be as well at this point to make it quite clear that a graphologist cannot foretell the future from handwriting. Only quacks would stoop to such a pretension in order to satisfy sensationalists and commercialize graphology.

Although indications of ill-health are expressed in writing illness cannot be diagnosed with accuracy. It is possible to discern the region of the body in which the disease lurks, and we may be able to recognize physiological changes, but we cannot be sure of an infallible diagnosis. We ought not to trespass beyond our domain, but we can co-operate with the medical profession by being able to recognize the psychological disturbances apart from the physiological ailment. Graphology can give valuable help to psychopathology as will be made evident in the course of this book.

In spite of obvious limitations more can be determined from handwriting than most people are prepared to know about themselves. Human nature is seen unadorned when it can be pinned down under a magnifying glass.

The knowledge of handwriting interpretation is not used to pry into private lives but to help men to a better mutual understanding and to enlighten them generally. A timely graphological analysis can ensure a step in the right direction, because the graphologist can see the effects of traits and symptoms shown in the writing. Misfits in marriage, in business and in the choice of vocation can to a large extent be eliminated if expert advice is taken.

In analysing handwriting many factors have to be isolated prior to the formulation of a report. The graphologist has first to determine the circumstances under which the script was written, the position of the writer and of the paper, the manner in which the pen was held and the nature of the writing materials. When all this has been found out the diagnosis of the writer's character can be begun. The choice of writing implements is not of course completely accidental but is due partly to the writer's character. And writing itself changes not only through the development of each personality but also through other causes. A penman may give testimony to his good visual memory by absorbing environmental influences for example. Again, if we examine our own handwriting, we see clearly that it changes not only at different times of the day but also under different conditions and according to our interest in the content of what we are writing. Increased interest, for example, makes the features of our writing less constrained, less controlled and more automatic. In the same way the beginning and the end of a script tend to be different. Initially a writer is inclined to be on his guard and to appear on his best behaviour; towards the end of his script he is more likely to 'let himself go'. That is why the end of a letter is more significant and of greater symptomatic value than its beginning. The beginning tends to show the role the penman would like to play, but the end reveals him in his true colours. It may also happen that a writer is inhibited at first and gains confidence only as he goes along, a situation which a graphologist would recognize and take into consideration.

During the last century the scientific study of handwriting has been gradually developing. Today one of the most reliable methods of interpreting it that is available to graphologists is by the technique of Dr. Robert Saudek.[1] According to Saudek the *speed* of a handwriting is the basis of every graphological analysis, and he worked out Tables of Speed[2] by which the quickness or slowness of handwriting could be accurately assessed. The next step of importance in analyzing handwritings is to judge their rhythm, the 'kinetic melody' as the famous neurologist, Professor von Monakow, calls it. Only after a study of speed and rhythm does the graphologist begin to isolate any elements of the writing before him.

The graphologist examines for his criteria the inconspicuous parts of a handwriting such as the middle letters with loops like f, h, g, j, y, and z, the width or narrowness of the other small letters and the divergence in spacing. He observes the margins and paragraphs, the space between lines which is called the vertical spacing, and the space between words which is called the horizontal spacing, and he notices the manner in which the diacritics (the i-dots and t-bars) are shaped and where they are placed.

When the various elements have been isolated and all the features dissected, the first part of the examination is done. The second part consists in making a synthesis of all the findings and reconstructing one harmonious whole from them. The final report should reveal a life-like picture of the analyzed person. It should not be a mere description but a logical building-up of the character-structure. It is therefore of paramount importance that the graphologist be familiar with the working of the mind. A sound knowledge of psychology, particularly of the analytical methods, is indispensable for all handwriting-analysts.

---

1 Dr. Robert Saudek, the well-known Czech graphologist, is internationally known through his books; *The Psychology of Handwriting* and *Experiments with Handwriting*, both published by Messrs. Allen and Unwin.
2 See Chapter I of this book, pp. 13-25.

INTRODUCTION

A certain amount of affinity between graphologist and writer is very helpful. Should the mentality of the writer be quite alien to the writing-analyst, there is some difficulty in formulating the report. The graphologist prefers also to analyse the writings of people he has never seen, for it is often difficult to 'square' what is known by slight acquaintance of a person's character with what can actually be observed in his writing. Graphological data alone are more reliable than a superficial knowledge of the writer.

Theodor Reik, the Viennese psychoanalyst, says in one of his recent books, *The Inner Experience of a Psychoanalyst*,[1] that the analyst must learn to listen with a third ear in order to be able to understand the unconscious processes going on in the patient. In the same way the graphologist must learn to see with a third eye in order to penetrate into the unconscious being of the penman. With this third eye he has access to the depths of human nature.

Analysing handwritings involves grave responsibilities. Nothing must be left to chance and the best safeguard against allowing intuition to run riot is a sound technique. Dr. Saudek's method can be tested, repeated and verified, and from this point of view graphology is not only empirical but also scientific. To throw more light on this subject we will begin with an explanation of Saudek's technique of analysis and show it in use in a full writing analysis.

---

1 Published by Allen & Unwin 1949.

CHAPTER ONE

Saudek's Technique

Handwriting, apart from being a means of recording our thoughts, feelings, decisions and communications to the outside world, is a kind of behaviour, revealing to the experienced eye of the graphologist the penman's individuality. First and foremost we are interested to know if a man is sincere or insincere, if he means what he says or if he merely plays a part, and if the latter *why* he playacts. One of the fundamental tasks of the graphologist is therefore to diagnose spontaneity and sincerity on the one hand and affectation and insincerity on the other.

Saudek holds that one of the principal indications which distinguish natural from unnatural handwriting is the writer's speed. Other things being equal, an unnatural affected hand is written more slowly than a spontaneous informal handwriting. The cornerstone of Saudek's technique is therefore the estimate of the rate at which a handwriting was produced.

In order to arrive at this estimate with accuracy Dr. Robert Saudek worked out tables of speed and slowness and laid down twenty-six rules by which to determine the rate at which a script was written. This estimate of speed forms the basis of every handwriting analysis and is our fundamental guide to the psychological comprehension of the writer.

Now speed may be due to one of several causes, to a vivacious temperament, to momentary emotion, to dynamic impulses or just to experienced penmanship. Slowness too is caused by various conditions: it may be due to the mechanical means of writing such as the paper, the pen or the ink, or it may be caused by depression or by a deliberate intention to deceive. We must note too that precisely the same signs may have completely different meanings in a quick and a slow hand. A slow writer producing certain marks in his script may be untruthful or even dishonest, whereas the same symptoms in a quick hand of a high standard merely show diplomacy or clever manipulations.

13

In the tables of speed[1] given in this chapter the reader will find Saudek's laws systematically grouped. These tables were based on experiments in handwritings which were independently carried out by students who were for the most part teachers in schools. These experiments partly confirmed and explained and partly modified the significance of previously observed indications of speed. The tables therefore give a reliable means of determining the rate at which a handwriting was produced.

In this connection it is of particular interest to take into consideration the research and experiments of F. N. Freeman in the University of Chicago.[2] According to Freeman the initial stroke of

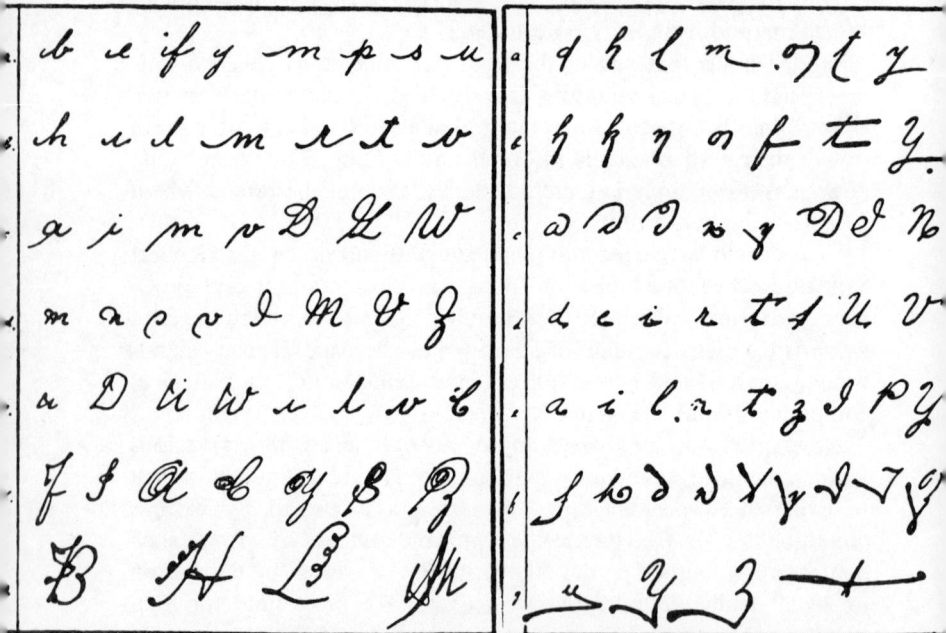

FIG. 1 · (Initial and Final Adjustments) FIG. 2

1 Tables of Speed and Slowness, from *Experiments with Handwriting*, R. Saudek (Allen & Unwin).
2 cf. *Experiments with Handwriting*, R. Saudek (Glossary).

the first letter is preceded by a shorter or longer period of adjustment to the task of writing. These adjustments are unwittingly recorded on the paper as a redundant stroke, a curve, a circle, a dot or a fish-hook. Examples are given in Figures 1 and 2.

These additional strokes are termed initial or final adjustments. The more elaborate of them require several time-units for their execution. so that a considerable waste of time is illustrated in them. They indicate the penman's deliberation, hesitation, uncertainty, hea· ‥ess, mental slowness or lack of discernment as the case may be. Adjustments of the more elaborate variety are incompatible with speed and show that the person concerned loses himself in futile activities.

The more quickly we write the more we join the letters of individual words without interruption. Even several words may be connected for the sake of quickness, since every disconnection entails a readjustment of the nib on the paper and a corresponding loss of time.

Note too that a meticulous penman dots his i's, while the swift writer dashes the dots across the paper, and may even join them to the next word.

By means of slow-motion cinematic pictures Freeman measured in units of a twenty-fifth of a second the length of time required to adjust the nib at the beginning of the writing movement, to execute an upstroke, a downstroke and a curve, to make an angular connection and so on. His object was to devise the most efficient time-saving type of cursive writing. The results of his experiments are therefore relevant to the assessment of the degree of writing-speed.

The following are Saudek's Tables of Speed and Slowness. They are followed by examples of handwriting that illustrate the points made in the tables:

TABLE I
Primary Signs of Quick Writing. (Plus)

1. Smooth and unbroken strokes and rounded forms.
2. Frequent signs of a 'tendency to the right' all through the manuscript, alternating with a 'tendency to the left' at the ends of lines where the end of the sentence occurs in the following line.

3. Great uncertainty of aim after temporary interruptions of the act of writing, i.e. after syllable or word impulses.

4. Increased continuity of action as the writing proceeds, e.g. the connection of diacritical signs with the following letter, the joining of numerals in the same group of figures and so on.

5. The curtailing and degeneration almost to illegibility of letters towards the ends of words.

6. 'Primarily wide' script, i.e. writing in which the distance between the strokes in letters like m, n, u, is wider than their height, especially in the case of vertical writing.

7. Great difference of emphasis between upstrokes and downstrokes.

8. Widening of the left-hand margin as the writing proceeds.

9. No initial or final adjustments.

TABLE II
Secondary Signs of Quick Writing. (Plus)

1.(*a*) Increasing obliquity as compared with the normal angle of a school copy.

(*b*) Increasing tendency to a reversed angle (over 90 degrees when the school copy was vertical) and to a lateral grip of the pen.

2. 'Secondarily wide' writing, i.e. writing in which the distance between the letters within words is wide, especially if the script is at the same time primarily narrow.

3. Rising lines though paper and pen are at normal angles.

4. Infrequent changes of the grip of the pen.

TABLE I
Primary Signs of Slow Writing. (Minus)

1. Wavering forms and broken strokes.

2. Frequent signs of a tendency to the left.

3. Conspicuous certainty of aim with scarcely perceptible deviations from the intended direction of motion.

4. Frequent pauses during execution, recognizable from meaningless blobs due to readjustments, angles, divided letters and unrhythmical separations within the

word itself (English script excepted) and touching-up of letters.

5. Careful execution of significant details of letter-forms, and amplifications of strokes towards the ends of words.

6. 'Primarily narrow' script, i.e. writing in which the strokes of such letters as m, n, u, are higher than their width, especially in slanting writing.

7. Hardly perceptible difference of strength in up-strokes and downstrokes, writing produced with very little pressure or pasty writing.

8. Ornamental or flourishing connections.

TABLE II
Secondary Signs of Slow Writing. (Minus)

1. Downstrokes parallel almost as in a school copy.

2. 'Secondarily narrow' writing, i.e. writing in which the distance between letters within words is narrow, especially if the script is at the same time primarily wide.

3. Sinking lines, well marked from the beginning of the line not only during the course of the line.

4. Frequent changes of the grip of the pen.

A short study of examples of writing will make these points clear.

The writing in Figure 3, for example, has all the marks of a skilled penmanship. It is legible in spite of simplifications and is completely natural. Even the untrained eye can judge that it is writing of a high standard. The letters forming the words are consistently connected while the size of the writing and the refined pressure show the tact of a modest academic personality.

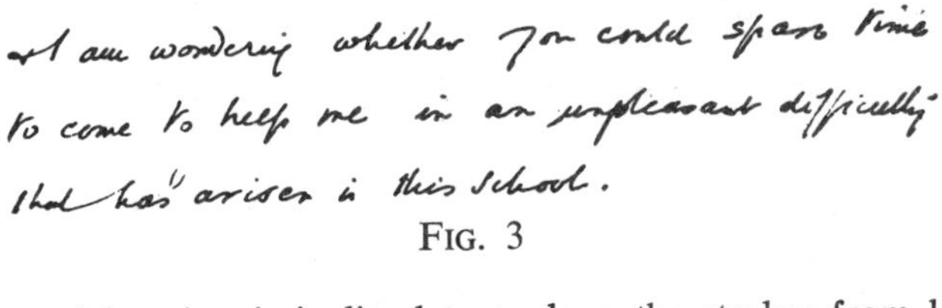

FIG. 3

The quick writer is inclined to prolong the strokes from left to right, yielding to his natural impulse. This inclination can be seen in Figure 4.

A handwriting that showed all the plus signs of the tables of speed would be extremely fast, even hasty. However, handwritings

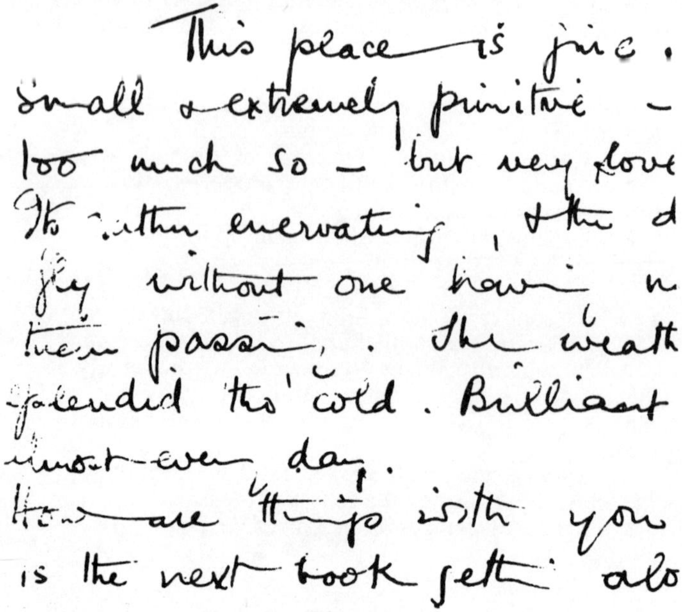
This place is fine.
small & extremely primitive –
too much so – but very love
It's rather enervating, & the d
without one
passing. The weath
splendid tho' cold. Brilliant
almost every day.
How are things with you
is the next book getting alo

FIG. 4

with all the symptoms of speed and without a vestige of restraint and inhibition are exceptional, nor are they desirable. From a practical point of view they would be illegible; from the psycho-

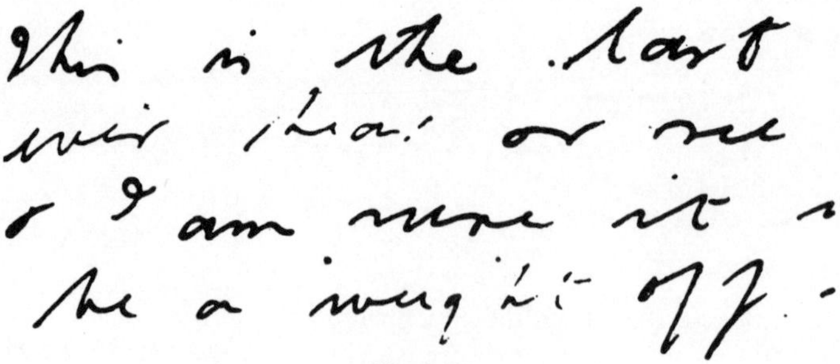
This is the last
or
I am sure it
be a weight off.

FIG. 5

logical point of view they would represent a type of behaviour indicating the extreme agitation of an unbalanced mind.

Figure 5 shows most of the signs of speed. There is a frequent tendency to the right, the diacritics are far above the stem, the ends of the words have degenerated to illegibility, the angle of writing increases from sixty degrees to forty degrees as the writing proceeds, the script is secondarily wide and the lines are rising. But we also find some of the slow signs of the tables of speed, such as trembling strokes, a pasty writing, i.e. one showing no change in the shading of up- and down-strokes, and a frequent change of the grip of the pen, which can be seen in the distribution of pressure in down-strokes and sidestrokes—always an indication of a moody and changeable person. This specimen approximates to habitually fast writing, but as it is illegible it defeats its practical purpose and indicates a deeply-seated restlessness, impatience and fickleness, which the writer is unable to control. She acts and reacts rashly on the spur of the moment without discretion or judgment and therefore cannot be relied upon, for she accomplishes little if anything of lasting value. (A more detailed account of this handwriting is to be found in Chapter 7 p. 107. (Inebriety).

Figure 5 gives us an instance of speed in its negative aspect then. Speed, however valuable and even essential if applied with moderation, must be under control if it is to be an asset, and control means some degree of retardation. In order to be really effective quick handwriting must show one or two of the signs grouped on the slow side of the tables of speed, because these slow signs indicate that the quick writer is exercising his will to curb his vivacity and his responsive disposition.

Not every one of the signs of slowness has the same value; each of them has a special function and significance of its own. Broken or trembling strokes, for example, (Minus I in the Tables of Speed) do not indicate control but suggest a severe inhibition and a lack of co-ordination.

Psychosomatic difficulties are well illustrated in Figure 6 which shows a very quick hand denoting acute nervous strain bordering on a breakdown. Morbid excitability, anxiety, fever, acute intoxication and disturbed states of body or mind are thus expressed in handwritings. Physical disability is sometimes responsible for slow writing, and spelling difficulties, as for example when writing in a

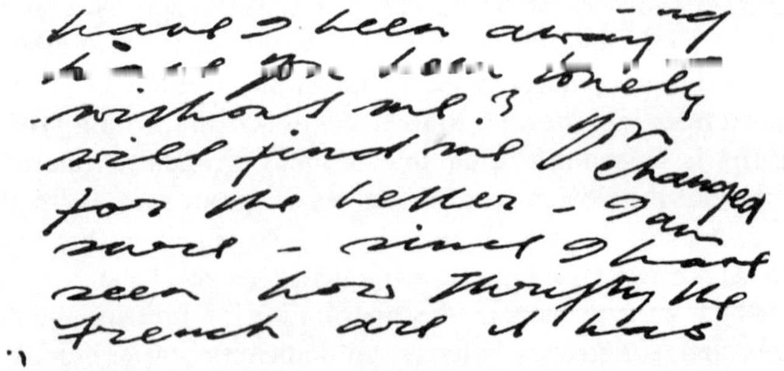

FIG. 6

foreign language, may give rise to reduced speeds. A similar effect may be produced when using a defective pen or smeary ink. When isolating these features only purely psychological causes of slowness in the writing should be considered.

Slow thinkers of phlegmatic temperament, plodding workers who cannot be hurried, have at their best a fair amount of reasoning and their knowledge is sound and their temperament even. They do not set the world on fire, but they are steady and reliable.

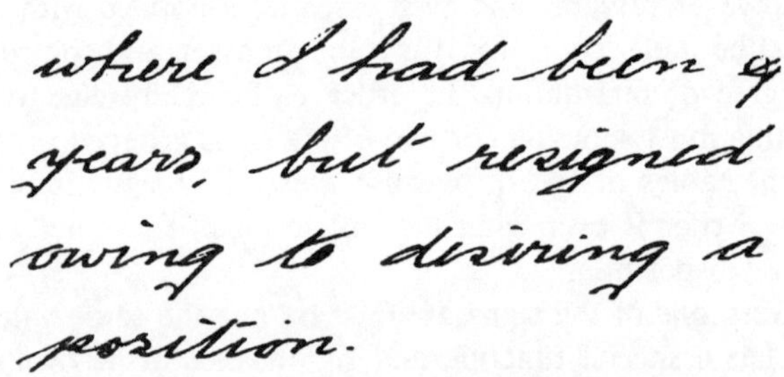

FIG. 7

Figure 7 shows many symptoms of slowness but at the same time a number of quick signs which are equivocal symptoms and must be considered slow in this particular writing. For example comma-shaped i-dots are not only due to haste and vivacity; they can also be due to laziness. A connected hand which is partly soldered, i.e. carefully joined so that an interruption should not be detected, is also a symptom of slowness. In Figure 7 we have a blatant example of an inert, primitive and incompetent man who lacks backbone and sincerity. He is slapdash and not commendable. The formation of the tail of the 'g's' give him away. He is not really trustworthy, but tries to grab what he can from life. But an example of the positive type of slow writer, steady and thorough, is furnished in Figure 8. The writing shows frequent signs of a tendency towards the left, frequent pauses during execution, accurately placed diacritics, meticulous execution of letter-details, narrowness and a few initial adjustments.

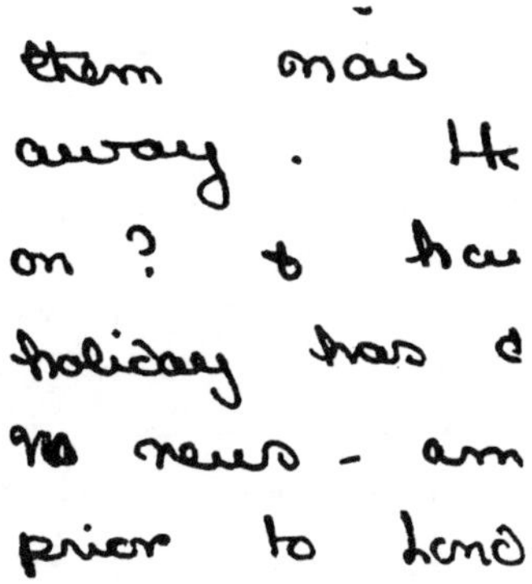

FIG. 8

If we compare the two specimens of slow writing we find that, in spite of many symptoms of slowness, Figure 8 shows more positive signs than Figure 7. The writer of Figure 8 may be slow, but she exerts herself in her methodical and circumstantial manner, whereas the writer of Figure 7 lacks energy and is sluggish and inert.

After estimating speed the next step in an anlysis is the observation of the spacing of a script. General spacing refers to the margins and paragraphs of a manuscript; inner spacing pertains to the vertical spacing, i.e. the space between lines, and to horizontal spacing, i.e. the space between words.

The sheet of paper represents the world in which we find ourselves, so that well-balanced spacing indicates that the penman adapts himself to the circumstances at his disposal.

In Figure 9 we have an example of almost perfect spacing which gives evidence of a person who knows how to avail herself of her

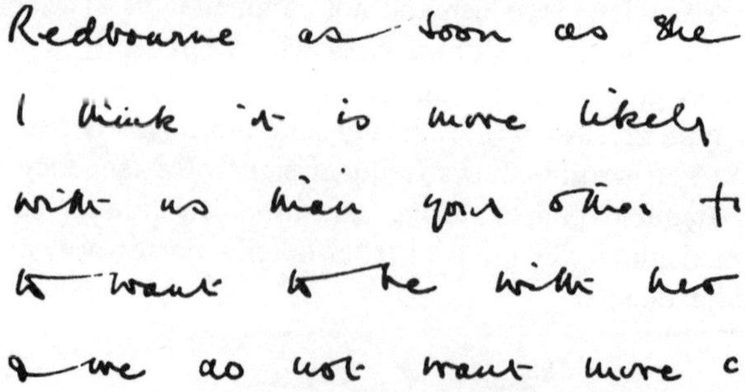

Redbourne as soon as the

I think it is more likely

with us than your other to

to want to be with her

I we do not want more c

FIG. 9

opportunities. The upper margin is aesthetic, the left margin is in keeping with the rest of the margins and is quite straight, and the writer makes good use of the space at her disposal and stops before she oversteps the mark.

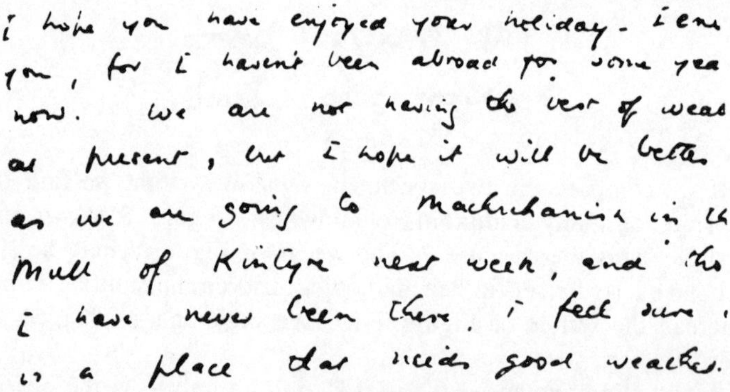

i hope you have enjoyed your holiday. I am

, for I haven't been abroad for some yea

now. We are not having the best of weat

at present, but i hope it will be better

as we are going to Machrihanish in the

Mull of Kintyre next week, and the

I have never been there, i feel sure.

is a place that needs good weather.

FIG. 10

In Figure 10 we note a straight left margin, which may be considered stylized. The horizontal spacing is evenly distributed right through the script and each word stands as a unit. The vertical spacing is very clear and denotes a lucid mind. The distance between lines and the distance between words illustrate how a methodical organiser avails himself of his space.

22

Figure 11 differs completely from Figure 10. In glancing at it we feel almost giddy because of the dazzling writing. The general

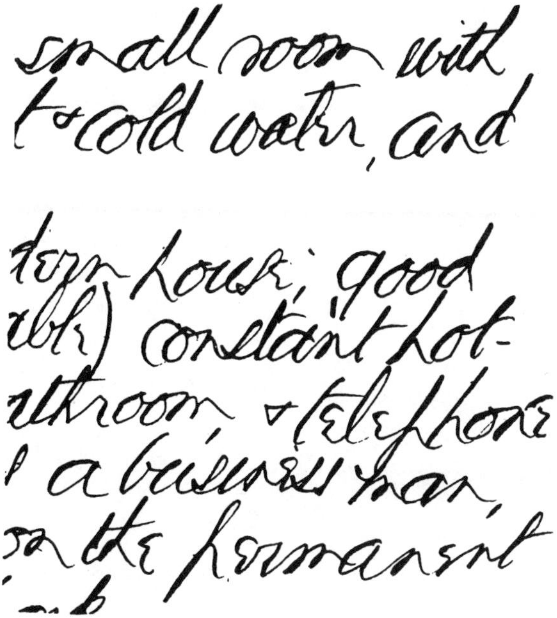

FIG. 11

spacing as well as the inner spacing is completely bewildering.

In Figure 12 we have exceptionally straight lines which indicate stability and a purposive striving towards a fixed goal.

Whatever the graphologist may determine from a study of speed and spacing will not have the force of evidence unless the 'standard class' of the penman is also ascertained. In his book, *Experiments with Handwriting*, page 249, Saudek says, 'The term "standard class" was deliberately chosen to signify the general intellectual level of a writer, the degree of his natural sincerity or his unnatural affectation, his originality or commonplaceness, his capacity for reactions to impressions, his aesthetic refinement, his vivacity or dullness, in short our valuation of what we call a personality.'

Saudek classifies handwritings into ten standards. The writing of

23

most people, however, usually ranges between standard two and standard eight, because it is hardly possible to find a personality

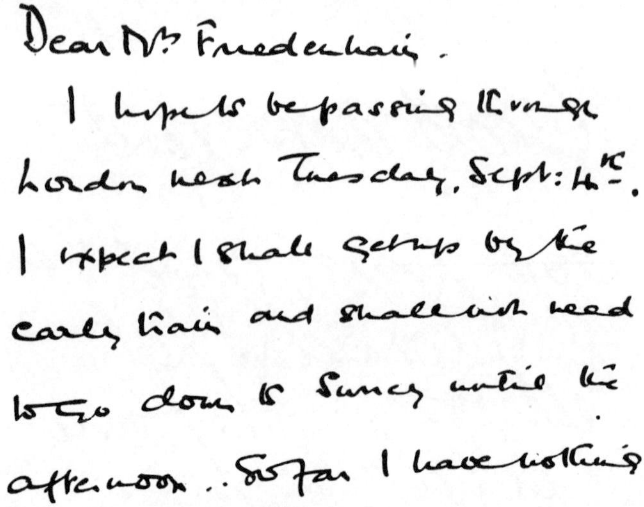

Dear Mr Friedenhain.

I hope to be passing through London next Tuesday, Sept: 4th. I expect I shall get up by the early train and shall not need to go down to Surrey until the afternoon. So far I have nothing

FIG. 12

so perfect as to be classified as standard one and fortunately we cannot find many handwritings pertaining to persons as bestial as to deserve standard ten. The standards, however, cannot be rigidly defined.

There are three criteria for the determination of standard class. They are first, the degree of speed and naturalness or unnaturalness of the writing; second, the general, horizontal and vertical spacing; and third, individual letter-formations which are given positive or negative value and on which characteriological conclusions are based.

The graphologist always studies the rhythm of a writing he is analysing. Rhythm is largely determined by the speed of writing and is easier to recognize than to define. Rhythm is the original fundamental form of vitality which oscillates in individuals. This cosmic throb exists in all natural beings; it swells our emotions, governs our feelings and rules our life. No rational measure is capable of gauging it and its flow is never exactly regular but it

24

runs like a stream through the world of our experience. We cannot determine rhythm with exactitude in handwritings but we can apprehend it intuitively. Before starting on any detailed examination of a handwriting this unknown quantity, which supplies the key to the ultimate secret recess of the soul, must be ascertained.[1] Figure 3 is a perfect example of rhythmical writing.

To sum up so far then: A quick, natural, rhythmical hand, well spaced, clearly legible and with original aesthetic shapes is produced by a writer of a high standard. (Figure 10 is a good example). Neglected spacing, irregular margins, dovetailing of the vertical spacing and letters of a primitive shape written in a slow hand are the work of a writer of low standard. (Figure 11 illustrates this type).

One of the most significant elements in handwriting is pressure. Max Pulver, the eminent Swiss graphologist, in his book *Symbolik der Handschrift*[1] devotes a most interesting chapter to pressure. 'Pressure,' he says, 'is the expression of an elementary necessity; it is the third dimension. Real pressure is a dynamic phenomenon, heavy strokes are merely mechanical. When we speak of real pressure we are mainly considering the effect of the pressure on the pen. The soft pen produces it without special effort on the part of the writer because there is no resistance. The hard pen is more complicated and more difficult to use. There is a difference between heavy strokes and pressure; both have to be interpreted according to their cause. Heavy strokes are produced by mechanical means viz. a broad soft nib. Real pressure is caused by means of pushing the pen into the paper, thus leaving a trace, a scratching in the paper. Pressure in the up-strokes instead of in the down-strokes is a systematic evasion of the normal shading of writing. Technically it is produced by the lateral hold of the pen. This displacement of pressure stands for the repressed libido.'

'Pressure is not merely a manifestation of a strong will,' says Pulver.[2] It lies much deeper and has a creative function. The term "libido" is more appropriate. The man of strong vitality uses

---

1 cf. Saudek's *Psychology of Handwriting* p. 126.
2 See *Symbolik der Handschrift* by Max Pulver, translated by the author. *Der Druck* p. 220. Orell Füssli Verlag, Zurich.

pressure, manifesting either physical, mental or creative power. The sexually brutal man, the primitive man of natural pushing power, the instinctive man, the working man who is unaccustomed to writing and the sportsman all leave traces of pressure in their hand writings. Likewise the man with a heavy hand and the man with a heavy heart, who may live under pressure, write with strong pressure. Courage, violent affectivity, obstinacy and a choleric temperament are also expressed in strong pressure.'

Not only pressure or lack of pressure should be observed but it is also important to note where the pressure lies. It may be initial or final pressure, and it may be genuine or feigned.

Initial pressure-emphasis can be seen in Figure 13. In this particular case initial pressure is an overcompensation for bodily inferiority, the writer being hunchbacked. Final pressure emphasis is shown in Figure 14, where it indicates extreme obstinacy and intolerance.

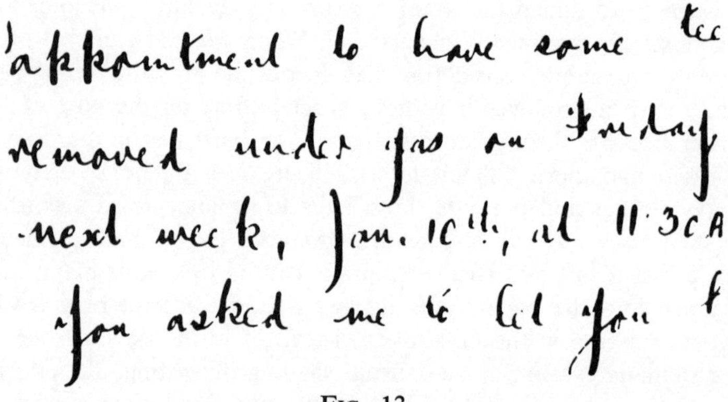

FIG. 13

Lack of pressure as shown in Figure 15 denotes a sensitive personality.

By way of contrast we see in Figure 16 arbitrary pressure produced by mechanical means. This is the writing of an artist who uses a quill.

In Figure 17 we have an example of pasty writing with no

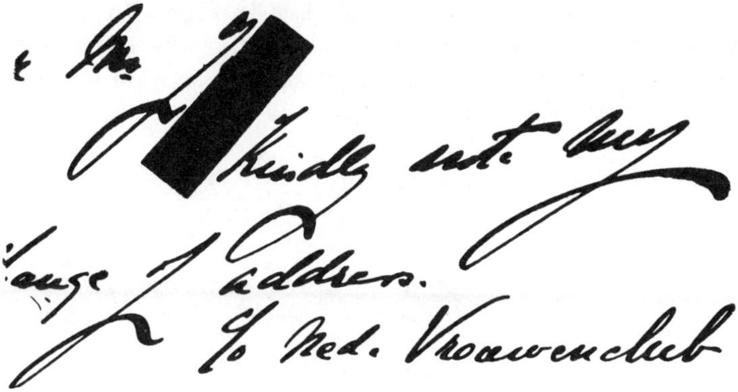

FIG. 14

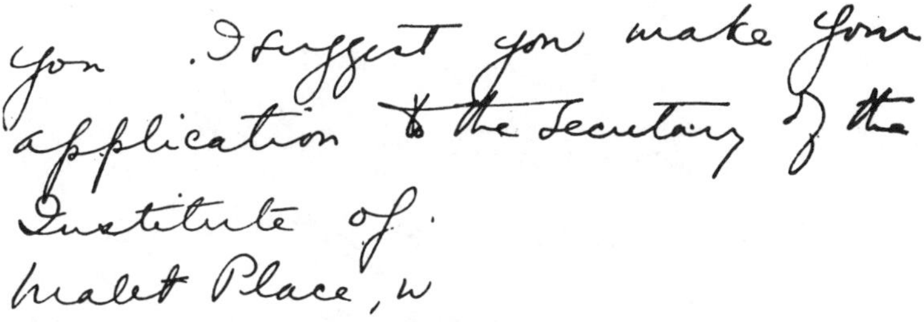

FIG. 15

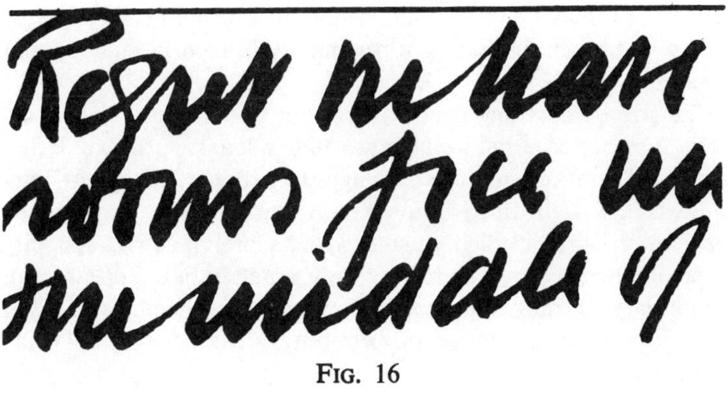

FIG. 16

difference between up- and down-strokes. In Figure 18 the heavy pressure of the heavy hearted person is seen.

The stroke of a handwriting has great significance for the graphologist. It may be fine and written by a sensitive and receptive

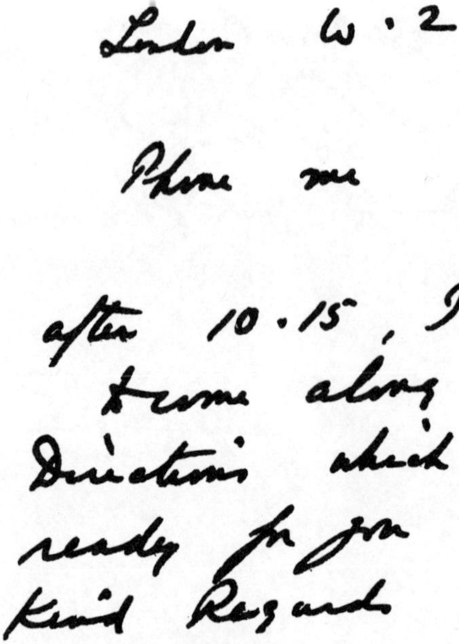

FIG. 17

person, or it may be heavy and written by a brutal person, or again it may be broken, indicating a personality broken in body or mind or both.

The size of a writing is also important in the interpretation of a script. For our criterion we take the middle letters such as a, i, m, n, into consideration and we distinguish between absolutely large handwriting, well fitted into the available space, signifying a spacious gesture justified by the writer's individuality, and large letters in other writing where they show an attempt to appear grand. Should large writing appear in a slow unnatural hand, as in Figure 19, it leaves the impression of an arbitrary character by no means genuine.

28

Small writing in a quick hand, as in Figure 10, shows power of observation, a capacity for concentration and objectivity.

Forms of connections reveal much to the graphologist, and the

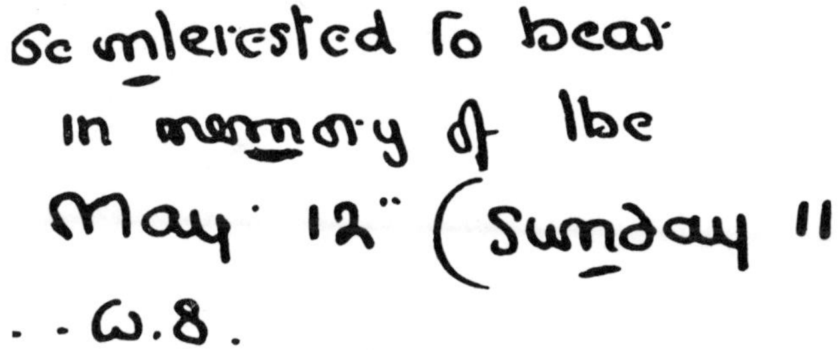

FIG. 18

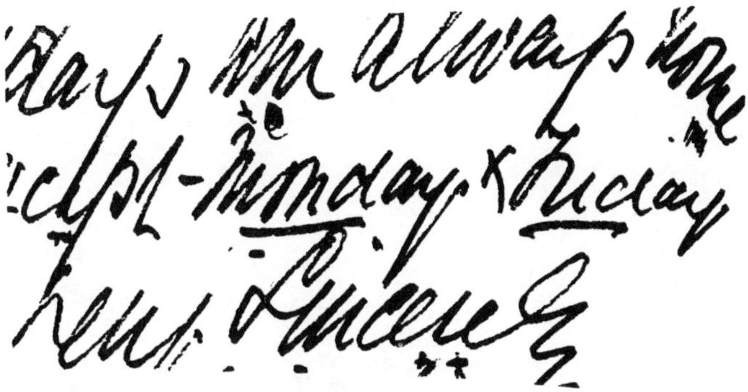

FIG. 19

reader will find the various forms of connection between the small letters of a writing illustrated in Figure 20.

Angles in a quick hand by a writer of high standard indicate quick resolution and determination. In a slow act of writing by a high standard writer angles denote perseverance, firmness and steadfastness of character. Angles in a slow hand of a low standard writer are a sign of harshness, inconsiderateness or obstinacy.

Arcades in a quick hand have no psychological significance, but in a slow hand they are a symptom of great secretiveness and, combined with three features of the dishonesty complex,[1] they denote untruthfulness.

---

1 For this complex see Appendix p. 179 (Mendacity complex).

Garlands in a quick act of writing of a high standard writer mean goodwill, kindness and sympathy in the writer's character. Garlands produced by a quick penman of a lower standard reveal a weak

Angles

Arcades

Garlands

Pseudo-garlands

Leftward-running half-ovals

Double-curves

Threads

Arcades & Double-curve

FIG. 20 :   Forms of Connections

compliant character which is easily influenced. If garlands are produced in a slow act of writing by a low standard writer we conclude that he is indolent and without moral resistance.

30

Reserve and dissimulation can be observed when pseudo-garlands (mechanical garlands) are the most prominent form of connections.

Leftward running half-ovals are the most incriminating symptoms of concealment.

Double curves in a quick writing develop into threads, but in a slow act of writing they signify indolence, evasiveness or a lack of moral fibre.

Thready connections, leading to deficient relief of the word-structure, are the most marked feature of general instability.

Arcades and double curves combined denote concealment.

Variations of all these sorts of connections show a lesser kind of lability and point to a lack of moral resistance and to instability.

Having studied the forms of all the connections in a script, the graphologist finally arranges the occurrence of the features of a writing into groups of signs all of which point in the same direction. If all the symptoms of a particular quality are present we are justified in saying that the writer certainly has this quality. However, this does not mean that the particular quality is pronounced in him. Such groups of signs afford an opportunity to confirm previous findings and to ascertain the finer nuances of the writer's mentality.

The technique of a handwriting analysis would be incomplete if we were to omit the grouping of characteristics pointing in the same direction into parallelisms termed complexes. All these complexes in alphabetical order can be found in the Appendix of this book.

In the next chapter we shall take a piece of writing and analyse it in detail as an example of the way in which the graphologist works using this technique.

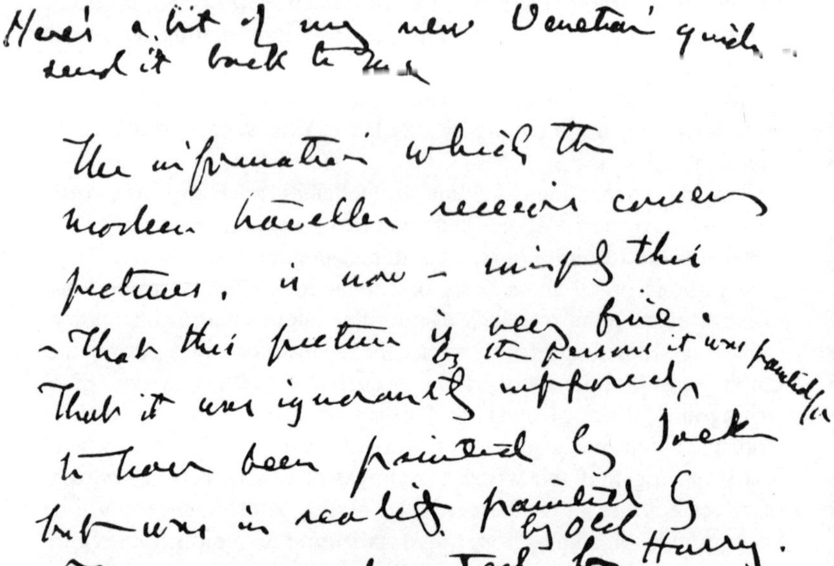

Here's a list of my new Venetian guide.
send it back to me

The information which the
modern traveller receives concerning
pictures, is now — simply this
— That this picture is very fine
That it was ignorantly supposed
to have been painted by Jack
but was in reality painted by
Tom, and repainted by old Harry.
and restored by Young Harry.
Who, with his beaver up,
calls on you — leaves his card.
and begs you to visit his studio —
— the old picture being really
now of very little consequence.
to either him — or you.

FIG. 21

A specimen of John Ruskin's handwriting.

32

CHAPTER TWO

A Handwriting Analysis

This specimen of John Ruskin's handwriting was chosen by the author to demonstrate the complete handwriting-analysis because opinions differ widely about Ruskin's character which is well portrayed in this specimen reproduced in Figure 21 opposite.

The reading of the text of the manuscript is the first step in the analysis. It runs, with all its corrections, as follows: —

Here's a bit of my new Venetian guide—
send it back to me.
The information which the
modern traveller receives concerning
pictures, is now—simply this
—That this picture is very fine.
That it was ignorantly supposed /by the person it was painted for
to have been painted by Jack—
but was in reality painted by
Tom, and repainted by Old Harry,
and restored /to splendid condition by Young Harry,
Who, with his beaver up,
calls on you—leaves his card,
and begs you to visit his studio—
—the old pictures being really
now of very little consequence,
to either him—or you.

Unfortunately this is not a full letter, but merely a note without signature. Thus an important part of Ruskin's personality is missing.

The next step in the analysis is the assessment of the speed of this writing. Some broken and atactic strokes may be observed as well as slight tremor, all of which are indications of a slow handwriting due to physiological causes. Therefore according to the tables of speed in Chapter I minus I is applicable.

Our natural direction in writing is from lfet to right. A writer who thinks more quickly than he can write and the natural outcome is that, driven by an inner impulse, he has a tendency to the right, which is speedier than a leftward tendency. The more intense the sentence-impulse, i.e. the uninterrupted flow of writing till the full stop is reached, the more impetuously a quick writer hurls the words on to the paper. We have a very pronounced tendency to the right in this script, so we have to mark it plus 2.

In spite of this forward-striving urge, we can plainly see frequent signs towards the left. We notice extended leftward strokes and leftward-turning lower projections (lower loops) not carried through to the right, e.g. line one *my*, line five *simply*, line six *very*. The word *reality* in line nine shows an exaggerated loop and a very marked leftward tendency. So the original tendency to the right is considerably modified by a tendency to the left, which we have to mark as minus 2. Thus early in our analysis we already have a clue that we are dealing with a self-contradictory nature.

The next criterion in assessing speed is the formation and placing of the diacritics. Nobody is able to write and place a dot correctly in a quick movement; i-dots in the shape of commas are more quickly produced and careless placing is easier than an exact position. It is important to note if the diacritics are placed high or low, to the right or to the left of the stem. In Ruskin's handwriting the diacritics are dashed on to the paper, many are omitted altogether, and some are extremely far to the right as in *Venetian*, line one. There is a very high t-bar in the word *repainted*, line ten. We therefore have a plus sign 3 for uncertainty of aim.

A quick writer produces a connected hand. Here again we see numerous contradictions in Ruskin. He certainly writes a connected hand, and even over-connects by joining several words together as in *tome*, line two, and *tohave* line eight, where the t-bar is connected with the h. In the fourteenth line *to visit his* shows an i-dot connecting with a t-bar which in its turn is connected with the next word while the t-bar of *to* connects that word with *visit*. In line sixteen two comparatively long words, *little* and *consequence*, are joined together by a prolongation of the t-bars to the first letter of the second word.

As the end of a manuscript has more symptomatic value than the beginning, we have to rate the connections of this writing higher than its disconnections, although we must not overlook the separations within words. We are therefore marking a *plus* 4, underlined to give emphasis to the over-connections, and a (minus 4) in brackets to indicate the pauses between letters in words. We see in Ruskin's hand not only a sentence-impulse but also a word-impulse and a letter-impulse, where the writing-movement is interrupted at the end of each letter. The capital H in *Here's* and the capital V in *Venetian*, line one, show a letter-impulse. *Information*, line three, shows a syllable-impulse, there being an immediate readjustment without a perceptible change of writing-movement after the syllable *in-*. *Ignorantly*, line seven, may also be considered as showing a syllable-impulse although the division of the word is not strictly in syllables. A certain amount of interruption in writing long words is of course essential; it represents the breathing-intervals during writing.

Now we look to see if the manuscript is carefully or carelessly executed, and we see that Ruskin does not finish his words carefully, but allows the letters to degenerate into illegibility towards the ends of words. This illegibility speaks for itself in Ruskin's letter; he obviously omits minor details in order to concentrate on important issues. The mark for this hasty execution is a plus 5. (Negligent letter-formation could denote sluggishness and laziness, but only in a low standard writing).

Next we determine the width or narrowness of the writing. Wide writing is done more quickly than narrow writing. We can clearly discern a wide hand in this specimen, for the distance between the down-strokes of the small letters such as n and m is wider than their height. This represents an additional sign of speed and gives us plus 6.

Now we examine the stroke of the writing. Pasty writing shows no difference in shading between up-strokes and down-strokes, but this specimen cannot be called pasty for there is a remarkably differentiated stroke in it, though this cannot be seen quite as clearly in the reproduction as in the original. We give this a plus 7 which denotes plasticity and flexibility of mind.

Plus 8 is the sign for an increasing left margin, and minus 8 denotes an ornamented or flourished hand. Neither can be seen in this script, so we pass on to the adjustments.

Initial and final adjustments retard the speed of a writing. Ruskin loses some fraction of a second in adjusting his pen to the paper, an indication of his friendly approach to his fellow-beings. But there are no noticeable final adjustments. We therefore have a plus 9 and a minus 9, the symptoms counterbalancing each other.

Secondary signs of speed or slowness increase or diminish the significance of the primary signs, so we next study the secondary signs to see what they tell us.

Secondary plus 1 stands for an increased angle of writing but the sign is not pertinent to this hand. The script does, however, show the wide writing termed secondarily wide (in which the distance between the letters within a word is wide), which is more quickly produced than narrow writing, so we mark it secondary plus 2. Rising lines are a sign of quickness and as they are evident in Ruskin's hand we note a secondary plus 3.

Should the writer change the grip of the pen frequently we find pressure in the down-strokes and in the side-strokes. This change of the grip of the pen, which denotes diminished speed, stands for irritability and capriciousness. Ruskin's note is full of irritability for the pressure of his pen runs in different directions. Thus we have a secondary minus 4.

Now we must summarize in a table all our findings on the speed at which this script was written. We get the following table:

Primary Signs of Speed

	Minus 1. tremulous and atactic strokes
Plus 2. tendency to the right	Minus 2. tendency to the left
Plus 3. uncertainty of aim	
Plus 4. connected hand	(Minus 4). disconnections
Plus 5. careless execution	
Plus 6. wide writing	
Plus 7. difference in up- and down-strokes	

Plus 9. no final adjustments   (Minus 9). slight initial adjust-
                                              ments
Secondary Signs of Speed
Plus 2. secondary width
Plus 3. rising lines

(Minus 4). change of the grip of
the pen

There are many signs of quickness, then, in this hand, but they
are slightly modified by a few signs of slowness, retardations due
to ill-health, self-recollection and irritability. Note that the mechanical means, the paper and the writing-implements, do not account
for any delay in this writing. The few slow signs, e.g. trembling
strokes, the tendency to the left and the initial adjustments, can be
explained as psychosomatic symptoms. It is clear that we are dealing with a fundamentally quick hand.

The standard class of this writer is high, for he is spontaneous in
his mode of expression, has a natural rhythm and produces unusually graceful shapes. The spacing is good, the left margin is
very straight, which is a symptom of aestheticism as well as of the
observance of convention, and the right margin is in parts well
arranged, showing that the writer tries to control his vivacity.

The vertical spacing, i.e. the space between the lines, is very
clear, a proof of Ruskin's clear thinking power. The lucidity of
thought appears slightly dimmed because of the frequent textual
alterations. The writer was undecided or had second thoughts as
he wrote and so revised and modified frequently.

The horizontal spacing, i.e. the space between words, is excellent, every word standing as a unit. This proof of a clear and
methodical mind counterbalances the corrections. The connected
words such as *tome, tovisithis, littleconsequence,* signify associative
thinking.

Altogether then, Ruskin's quick natural writing, well-spaced and
with aesthetic letter-formations, leads us to decide on standard
class 3.

The pressure applied by Ruskin is marked and denotes energy,
a hasty temper and a certain amount of tension. His small hand is
due to a power of concentration and good observation.

37

Varying size-ratios between middle letters, upper projections and lower projections diminish legibility and are a sign of inconsiderateness towards the reader. The size-ratios here vary considerably, a symptom of sensitiveness and capriciousness. Irregular variations of the writing-angle point in the same direction for they stand for an unbalanced temperament and changeable moods.

To complete the anlaysis we arrange the graphic indices that point in the same direction into parallelisms or complexes[1] of features. This gives us an opportunity of checking our previous findings. If these complexes or groups of features enable us to come to the same conclusions as we have come to by considering single items, the scientific side of the analysis is emphasized. By means of these constellations of features we eliminate errors as far as humanly possible, and at the same time we gauge the finer nuances of the character. Even with the minutest and most thoroughly examined data it is possible to misinterpret character sometimes. The technical part of the analysis is worked out through the subjective personality of the graphologist; the formulation of the report must be left to his psychological understanding. The creative building-up of the character, the synthesis which makes our work so interesting, is the result of our intuition and psychological knowledge combined. Crepieux-Jamin is right when he says, 'Graphology is essentially a science; in the practical application, however, it is an art and will always remain an art.'

Let us now consider the complexes or parallelisms of signs in Ruskin's handwriting.

The most outstanding feature in this script is indicative of *aesthetic criticism*.[2] The graphological signs are: simplifications, original letter formations, good inner and outer spacing, originality in connections, refined but resolute pressure. The psychological implications of this complex are: a love of beauty, refinement, artistic taste, originality and creative power.

The next complex pertinent to Ruskin's handwriting is *mental activity*.[2] The graphological indications are: several signs of speed,

1 The list of complexes is given in the appendix.
2 Appendix p. 1.
3 Appendix p. 3.

variability in the shaping of characters, in size, size-ratios and width, changes in the grip of the pen, simplifications as well as some enrichments and originality of characters. The psychological interpretation is: impressionability, original ideas, sensitiveness, moodiness, lack of balance and inner contradictions.

These two complexes would give us an idea of Ruskin's character in a nutshell, unless we were to find them counterbalanced by self-control. But as a matter of fact we find all the symptoms of *lack of self-control,* viz.: an irregular writing-angle, variability of style, careless execution of letter-formations particularly in inconspicuous parts, primarily wide and secondarily wide writing and uncertainty of aim.

Two symptoms of this complex are missing, for Ruskin has no sloping hand and his spacing is good. We shall have to find the reason for signs that contradict the complex of lack of self-control. The reason is embedded in the complex of *criticism.*[1] The symptoms are: simplifications, good spacing, a certain originality in connections and character-formation, (irregularity is possible when outbalanced by a certain amount of harmony, e.g. no emphasis of size-ratios, some symptoms of regularity and some consistency), no large script, neither extreme speed nor extreme slowness and a natural handwriting. The psychological deductions are: a sense of proportion, matter of fact sense, objectivity and a sense of humour.

We have then to build our estimate of Ruskin's character around these four main complexes, viz.: aesthetic criticism, mental activity, lack of self-control and self-criticism. It must be stressed that some aspects of affection, idealism, convention, vanity, ambition, energy, quick judgment and observation, sensitivity, courage and irritability have to be woven into the pattern to complete the picture.

Here then is our sketch of Ruskin's character based on the foregoing analysis:[2]

The rhythm of Ruskin's writing conveys to us the certainty that he is an outstanding personality. To apply normal rules for assessing any individual above the normal presents difficulties; they are,

1 Appendix p. 174.
2 Ruskin's handwriting was analyzed entirely by means of the specimen at the beginning of this chapter, but some information on his spacing was obtained from a few letters seen at the British Museum.

however, surmountable, for underneath the genius is the man with all his human frailties and weaknesses.

Knowing that we are in the presence of a truly challenging personality and dealing with an unusual phenomenon we shall be even more careful in our scrutiny than when confronted by our equals.

Ruskin thinks of himself as upright in character, noble of soul, a seeker after truth and justice, a moral fighter for a righteous cause. But he has an unbalanced temperament and cannot always produce positive reactions, so we have to consider fully his negative aspect, searching for the unconscious motives of his actions. Why does he fight? What is he fighting? Is the fight for the sake of ethics or is it due to an urge to overcome his own difficulties and conflicts? We can see that he has a continual struggle to accommodate his diabolic and his celestial dispositions, that he makes repeated attempts to reach the magnanimity which he pursues as his ideal. His equilibrium is disturbed in impression and in expression and therefore his life is a struggle from beginning to end. He must fight to conquer his own conflicts. Restlessly driven, he avoids quiet contemplation which he fears will overwhelm him. He has a great deal of innate energy at his disposal, and a dynamic force drives him to endless activities and social contacts, but all the time he is trying to escape from reality and from himself. He is fond of controversy, and yet at any given moment is ready to protect the weak. He is a brilliant conversationalist, in fact he needs an audience, but he makes a poor listener. He is endowed with a singular charm of approach and a sarcasm that can be captivating, yet he can be blunt and outspoken at times in an impulsive and uncontrolled manner that is painful to endure. He is strikingly demonstrative and eloquent, but nevertheless retains an egocentric reserve.

Why does Ruskin seek for truth? It seems as if he cannot find it within himself and therefore tries to escape from himself to seek it elsewhere. His relation to truth is unreal, his reality distorted. He loves the bizarre, the contradictory, anything phenomenal; there he finds a reflection of his own conflicts.

An unusual sensitivity, a penetrating ingenuity and a clear plasticity are interwoven in Ruskin's handwriting. He is many-sided, of extraordinary intellectual vivacity and has brilliant 'brainwaves' giving rise to sharp witticisms. He loves everything beautiful in art and nature with a love that is deeply rooted in him and that forms part of his religious sentiment.

If impressive issues are at stake Ruskin will overlook minor details for the sake of the final outcome. He is quick and determined in forming an opinion and not afraid to stand by it and defend it, for he has the courage of his convictions. He is, above all, a man of courage at all times and in all places, and, guided by pity and charity, will rally readily to the defence of the oppressed with delicacy yet with forcefulness.

Ruskin is unusually imaginative; in fact a self-deceptive illusion could even lure him into confusion. It is not unusual for him to lose his foothold for he lacks a practical mind and a sense of reality. Although he has a gift for organization he is not really methodical.

Analytically minded and empathetic, he is not fully explicit in expressing himself but inclined to forget that his fellow beings do not possess a power of comprehension equal to his own. He cannot endure fools gladly, is impatient with them and intolerant of their shortcomings. In the same measure he practises self-criticism, even to the extent of being harsh towards himself. His self-accusations, however, do not lead to constructive achievements, but more often than not to bitter resentment. In contrast to an unbending tenacity of purpose, his impressionability and his compassion betray an almost feminine disposition. He is used to being authoritative and dictatorial, an attitude which at its best takes a protective turn. Proudly convinced of the stir and sensation he can produce he likes to make a dramatic entry.

On the one hand he shows signs of the pampered child who has had a lavish upbringing, on the other an undue amount of tension which is the outcome of a frustrated childhood. These contradictions are reflected in a vivid imagination and in a clipped mode of expression. Unity and harmony are inadequate in his mental make-up. Part of his personality is uncommonly young, almost immature, but the rest is adult, austere, puritanical and ascetic.

The writer of this script must have often found himself in great difficulties of his own making, for he sets to work in an irrationally impulsive manner, carried away by his artistic temperament, without considering the final consequences of his actions. An introspective nature impedes his rhythm and halts him while his impulsive energy urges him on conflicting purposes are always at play. Ruskin shows that he has charm and amiability but that he adheres to convention. His revolutionary nature is repressed for the sake of ingratiating himself with others, not always the best thing for the creative power of an artist. But though the philosopher and the artist are always in conflict, a sense of humour comes to the rescue and Ruskin can be very stimulating and entertaining.

The specimen for examination is undated and the date of its origin is unknown, but there are signs that it was written in the prime of Ruskin's life. A letter of 1863,[1] when Ruskin was forty-four, has great similarity of style to the script analyzed here. Ruskin's style of writing never changed considerably, except during periods of illness when marked disintegration set in.

The restless excitability, irritability and changeable moods that Ruskin shows, the fact that a calm equilibrium rarely pervades his mind, give testimony not only of human frailties but of a highly-strung and sensitive nervous system and an inferior state of health. Severe inner conflict inhibits his instinctive drives. Fear of sensuality and of sexual demands is backed by wilfulness which is prominent in Ruskin's character. He is afraid of himself or of something within himself. An urge for a liaison is consciously pressing forward, and yet Ruskin is unable to form a close relationship with one of the opposite sex. Thus he is finally resigned to a denial of love and friendship, a disappointment in his emotional make-up. By bringing the higher virtues of his inner life into play he tries to overcome instinctive perversions.

Ruskin has a very high ego-ideal and the awareness of his unworthiness compared with this ideal results in a religious, devotional sentiment. The discrepancy between the claims of his conscience and his actual achievements causes tension and a feeling of guilt which at times has a paralyzing effect. Morbid sensitiveness and depressive brooding are the outcome of an inadequate outlet for

---

1 Letter at the British Museum.

his instinctive drives which become intellectualized in the mysterious and the supernatural.

Whether Ruskin is genuinely religious is difficult to determine. Religion appears to be the sublimation of his lower urges, but he certainly has enthusiasm, idealism, awe and reverence. However, as he is completely undogmatic, we could infer that he is an honest doubter. A man who is sustained by faith in a high power and in human nature is in harmony with himself and with his universe. Ruskin seems to be denied both these sources of harmony. He takes it into his own hands to reorganize the world and must prove to himself that he is sincere about it. In revaluing the values he throws overboard everything which once seemed good to him and attempts to live in contrast with his former self.

Change of occupation, change of friends, change of social and religious views; Ruskin changes everything in the hope of attaining peace of mind. He has the most dangerous revolutionary within himself and thus runs the risk of losing himself. He is far too haphazard in the expenditure of his emotions and lacks a sense of proportion when giving his affections, being sometimes lavish with his feelings and sometimes lacking in a warm response to love. There are, however, outstandingly good features in his character, a reverent devotion to art and beauty, to aestheticism and to nature, and a social conscience and dedication to humanity which are interwoven in his nature like a precious thread.

CHAPTER THREE

Graphology in the Service of Human Relationships

Shaping the lives of other people is a serious responsibility. Experience has shown, however, that graphology can play its part in advice about human relationships and in educational and vocational guidance. Many disappointments in life could in fact be avoided by means of a timely handwriting-analysis.

Some examples of advice about human relationships will give evidence in this chapter of the significant role of graphology. Unfortunately none of the author's work with regard to marriage can be included as the delicacy of the matter forbids it, but other family relationships and friendships are included. Each sample of writing was fully analyzed in the way shown in Chapter II but the analysis is not given here.

Our first case concerns Grace who was aged 17, and whose writing can be seen in Figures 22 and 23. She was extremely moody and an analysis of her handwriting showed her to be deeply depressed. A graphological analysis can penetrate to the depths of human nature even in its darkest hours, and this is the report on Grace.

The writer is an amiable girl, whose adroit manner is an asset

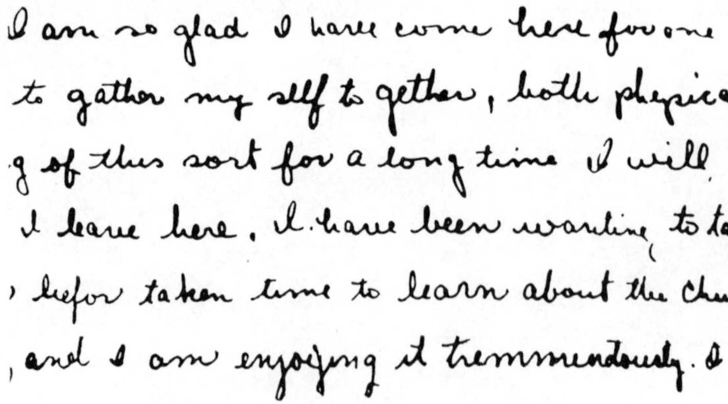

FIG. 22

44

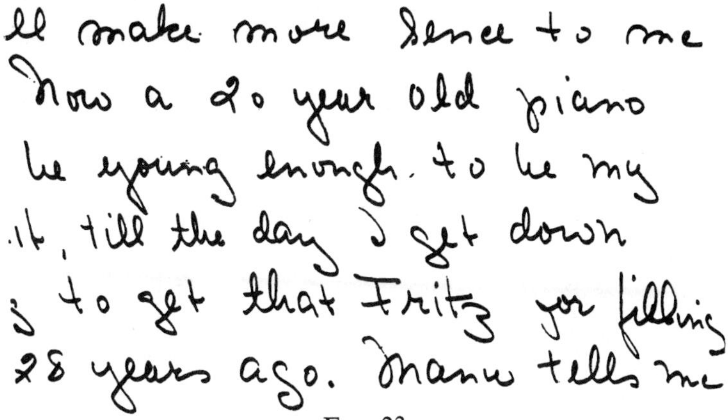
ll make more sense to me
now a 20 year old piano
be young enough to be my
it, till the day I get down
to get that Fritz for filling
28 years ago. Mama tells me

FIG. 23

to her in her adjustment to circumstances. Life seems to have played havoc with her emotions. In these specimens of her writing is expressed a cramped self-restraint quite unlike her natural mental make-up. Grace is actually an adventurous type of girl, the sort that does not take root anywhere. But here, there is a clinging to the sheet of note-paper which symbolizes Grace's world, and this expresses a clinging to someone or something abstract such as an idea or an ideal. It seems to be a pitiful cry for help and security. Observe her 'I' symbolizing the ego. It denotes an S.O.S. for friendship and protection and suggests the writer does not consider herself fit to live. She is in fact still a mere child, helpless and immature, and she has been forsaken by her mother. In many ways Grace is far too infantile for her age, but in others she is too far advanced. She needs an outlet for her tender emotions, for although they are completely repressed at the moment her true nature breaks through at times.

There are times when Grace is able to convince herself of her own value. Sometimes she is apt even to over-rate herself, exaggerating her abilities in the same exaggerated fashion with which she shows dejection at other times. She is smart in repartee and fond of showing off. She does not feel a repentant sinner. On the contrary, she sometimes thinks of herself as superior to her fellows.

She is a creature of moods, sometimes feeling acutely depressed, forlorn and suicidal, but at others feeling smart, lively and able to impress those around her with her superiority.

Grace has a sensitive personality which always reflects the influence of the moment, This impressionability and the desire for its expression are the root causes of her changeable moods. She lives on her emotions and because she is anxious to attract attention and admiration she works herself into a state of tension. This is by no means a conscious effort but it is all the same a tax on her highly-strung nervous system. The strain causes a nervous exhaustion which leads to undisciplined behaviour, and the outcome of her disunity is a disharmony of action that is hampering her. It is of course impossible to expect complete harmony at this precarious age, but Grace's marked lability suggests the unbalanced temperament of a psychopathic case. Insufficient stamina to resist temptation drags her into the depths despite herself. At the time of writing Grace is fighting a deep depression and her whole personality is bent down under the weighty feeling of guilt. When she tries to lift herself to higher spheres she escapes harsh reality only by going into an illusory world of make-believe. From that world she is flung back into the real world which does not understand her and her difficulties

So Grace lives in extremes, swayed by idealism one moment materialism the next, and incapable of finding the mid-course of normal conditions.

Grace's statements are never quite accurate for they are coloured by the state of her mind at any given moment, and she is inclined to indulge in rhetorical expositions not altogether free from hypocrisy. Indolence is at the very core of her nature, and for a girl of her mentality it is a great danger. The chance of living in comfort and luxury without having to work for it would be bound to lure her into temptation, although she would put up a good fight against it. The struggle would not be strong enough, however, to counterbalance her innate inertia.

Should Grace have to work for her living she would be able to do only an easy job in order not to draw too heavily on her physical and moral resources. She is mostly interested in the externalities and vanities of life, so her occupation might be found in the world of fashion in some such work as dressmaking, millinery or window-dressing.

The report ended there. The known sequel to the case is as follows:

At the age of twenty-four Grace married a man double her age. For a time all went well and she seemed to develop into a conscientious housewife and companion. Four years after the marriage Grace's husband left for the continent and did not return. Both partners made new attachments so divorce seemed the only solution. Then, when she was left lonely once more and felt desperate, Grace decided to visit her mother in Switzerland, though she had not seen her for fourteen years.

In the meantime Grace's mother had married for the second time. Her husband was a man considerably younger than herself. When they met, Grace's step-father could not resist her charm and fell in love with her. Attracted by the same type of personality which had fascinated him in Grace's mother and unable to resist the lure of youth and beauty with it, he decided to divorce his wife and marry his step-daughter. Grace, unconsciously taking revenge on a mother who had deserted her when she badly needed her, felt quite justified in reciprocating her step-father's advances and finally married him. It makes sordid reading indeed.

The next case concerns two middle-aged ladies, Miss C. and

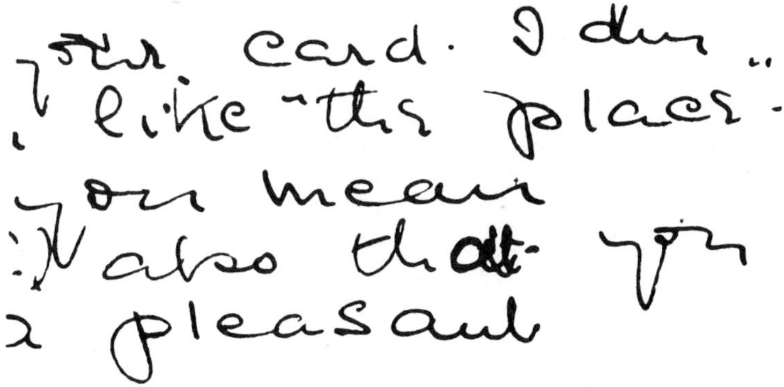

FIG. 24

Miss E., whose writings can be seen in Figures 24 and 25. These two women contemplated living together, but before making a decision Miss E., the writer of Figure 25, asked for graphological advice. To determine the mutual reactions three analyses were required, one of each partner and a third to ascertain to what extent their temperaments blended.

In the writing of Miss C., aged 54, (figure 24), we see a lady at the age of the climacteric and suffering from all its implications. Emotional instability is her keynote. This is the time when Miss C. is preparing life's balance sheet with its debit and credit sides. She is convinced that not much more can be expected from life and therefore she takes refuge from cold reality in a world of fantasy. Her upbringing is largely responsible for her attitude to life. She had an easy childhood, never learned to discipline herself, and now at a difficult period she considers herself fully entitled to act without restrictions. She lacks energy for any sort of work physical or intellectual. It is in fact owing to her inertia that she has not attained a higher cultural standard.

Every new situation flusters Miss C. who always fears that it will turn out for the worse. She is therefore reluctant to make a change. She is highly neurotic and has all the characteristics of her type, suspicion, doubt, envy, egotism, uncertainty and a feeling of inferiority. The result is a craving for power and self-assertion and an endeavour to make her influence felt. She has a generous trait in her nature but she expects a great deal in return for what she gives and is disappointed if she does not get all she anticipated.

Miss C. is expansive and fills the place wherever she is. Her changeable moods reflect nervous impatience at one time and such remarkable poise at another that one might even get the impression of a well-balanced harmonious personality.

Her present condition forms a superstructure over Miss C.'s real self and overshadows her true character. To avoid responsibilities she is only too ready to be taken care of. When feeling protected she might be affectionate for she is innately kind, which is definitely a redeeming feature.

Miss E. is 50 and a nurse by profession. Her writing can be seen in Figure 25 and the report on it was as follows:

48

Miss E. is exceptionally free from selfishness and particularly suited to help people with the right word at the right moment. Her sense of humour bridges many an unpleasant incident and, as she

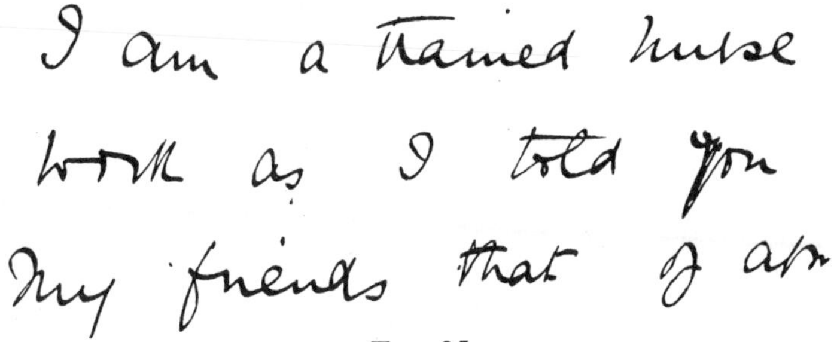

I am a trained nurse

work as I told you

my friends that I am

FIG. 25

is endowed with the gift of seeing the funny side of life, she often saves a difficult situation. She is methodical and energetic, and self-discipline directs her actions. She has a moody and irritable disposition which is not always easily overcome but severe self-criticism helps her to harmonize her personality.

Miss E. is hyper-sensitive, and when her feelings are hurt she takes a considerable time to recover. In spite of being shy and modest she lays down the law and means to see it obeyed. She is of a reticent, introspective and reserved disposition and does not attach herself to casual acquaintances; however once she has 'opened up' she is a true and sincere friend.

The writer is exceptionally well-suited for her profession, for she has a sympathetic understanding of her fellow-beings. Intuition, a gentle manner, refined tact and objectivity are outstanding features in her character.

Now, how do the temperaments of these two women blend? Could they share a home in a happy partnership?

Two more different temperaments could hardly be thrown together. This is, however, no criterion for supposing that the experiment must fail. Miss E. is of a gentle disposition, Miss C. is made of sterner stuff. The former is introspective and loves solitude, the latter is talkative and gushing without being stimulating. Miss E. has social interests and likes to work concentratedly, Miss C. is inert and almost asocial. From these differences it might be concluded that a shared home is not likely to lead to peaceful conditions. It will certainly not be on a basis of give-and-take as is usually expected of a comradeship, but it will have to be a giving-up of herself on the part of Miss E.

Miss C., though troublesome in many ways owing to her neurotic disposition, is not so much a bad as a trying person. Should Miss E. be prepared to accept her as a patient the relationship would be put on a different footing and it would be more possible to make it work satisfactorily. It would be a hard task for Miss E. but it would bring some compensation in return.

The report ended there, but the graphologist learned that under the circumstances Miss E. decided not to become a partner with Miss C. in a shared home.

The next case is that of Elsie, aged 23, whose writing can be seen in Figure 26. A young man whose friend she was asked for the handwriting analysis. He wanted an assurance of her sincerity. This is the report:

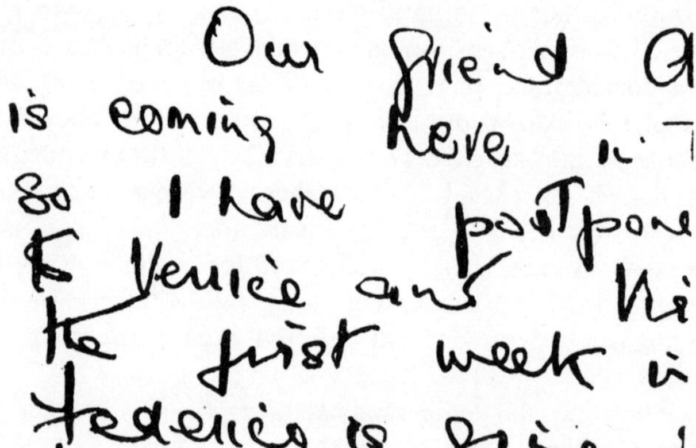
Our friend A
is coming here
so I have postpone
Venice and
the first week in
Federico is going

FIG. 26

Elsie, a young woman of charm, with amiable, lively manners, has great fascination. She is highly cultured and endowed with refined taste, having many intellectual interests in art and literature. Aestheticism is a necessity to her. She has all the potentialities of an original and creative mind, alert vivacity, quick-witted repartee and a lively imagination. She is a brilliant conversationalist and has a light savoir-faire which has carried her through life. She is well-informed and practical so that she is capable of managing her own affairs which she pursues first and foremost. A clear head for business and money matters stands her in good stead. Although she is a smart worldly-wise woman in the true sense of the words, she has a pronounced masculine streak in her make-up.

In spite of appearing communicative Elsie is secretive whenever it is to her advantage. Original ideas and all sorts of ingenious devices find a way for her out of the most complicated situations.

There are many contradictions in Elsie's character. Though she is highly-strung, easily excitable and of a very delicate nervous structure, the young lady can at times be aggressive and her sarcasm can be biting. These reactions are unpredictable and may occur when least expected. Tact and refinement, however, guard Elsie from serious outbursts. She knows what she owes to her good upbringing and to her prestige which she values highly. Brought up in a stylish home Elsie seems now to be at a loose end and very unhappy. Vitality and an adventurous spirit drive her forward but self-recollection puts on the brake.

Undoubtedly the temptations that come the way of an attractive bachelor-girl are numerous, but Elsie always fights to uphold the standards of her conservative background. Up to now she has managed to resist, but the price of her success is paid in restlessness, sharpness and a yearning for the fulfilment of her strong erotic urges.

It is advisable not to count on Elsie's faithfulness and sincerity, for she demands many changes for her happiness. She is fundamentally of a sweet and kind disposition but she is a born actress who always plays her part to perfection. She likes a good love-game and enjoys attracting and rejecting just for the sake of amusement.

What the young man did when he received this report is unknown, but, at least, he had been warned of possible difficulties in the relationship, and could weigh against them the good points in the young woman's character and abilities.

CHAPTER FOUR

Educational Guidance

Children often present problems to their parents or teachers, and sometimes those in charge of them are wise enough to consult those skilled in child guidance, psychotherapy or graphology. In this chapter will be found a few cases where educational guidance on a basis of a handwriting analysis was sought by a parent or teacher.

The first case is that of Freddy, aged 9, whose writing can be seen in Figures 27 and 28. Freddy's father applied for an analysis of his son's handwriting and this is the report given to him:

Freddy is an exceptionally intelligent boy, well advanced and more mature than is usual for his age. His vivacity is stimulating but his active mind and his impulsive reactions are apt to create difficulties for him. He is a brilliant boy who cannot conform to pattern but must follow his own laws of development. Intellectually he is free and at his ease; emotionally he is constrained and hampered by inhibitions. The boy has a truly lovable nature, is kindhearted, affectionate, understanding and highly sensitive to atmosphere. A vibrating restlessness and the unsettling conflicts of his age are expressed in Freddy's handwriting. He has many original ideas and can with bold directness hit the nail on the head when he wants to. He is a queer mixture of a thorough, almost pedantic boy and one who is easy-going and negligent.

Although we cannot expect complete harmony in a boy of nine, the irregularities in this handwriting suggest unusual difficulties. For example, the word 'underneath' in line 5 is well-formed compared with 'My' in line 10 which, although only a two-letter word, is irregular in size, width and angle, and looks as if it were the effort of a child who had just learned to write. In this letter there are many other striking examples which portray a brilliant boy inhibited by conflicts.

Freddy's writing is connected, though some of the characters are soldered. Look at the word 'sending' in line 2. The word appears to form a unity yet the 'e' is artfully joined to the 's', the 'd' is soldered to the 'n' and the 'i' is not actually connected with the

Dear Uncle Francois

you're Knife is very nice.

Thankyou for sending it.

I can draw it and
I will do it. It is right
underneath

The Pen Knife

It came
a bit late
but it does

not matter as long as it gets
here. My 2 brothers and father think
it is marvellous but I do not
let & my mother use it
in the R Real kitchen.

FIG. 27

'ng'. Freddy can obviously bluff to perfection. His writing shows many covering strokes which suggest inhibitions and untruthfulness, particularly when used in conjunction with arcades and double curves. His 'I's' are elongated indicating an ambitious nature and one that loves the limelight, yet some of those 'I's' are crossed through, showing that the writer is far from pleased with himself and sometimes feels inclined to cross himself out of existence.

Freddy's difficulties appear to be rooted in his family relationships. Observe the words 'My two brothers' and 'father' in line 10 and 'mother' in line 12. Freddy is the eldest of three. Doubtless he has felt displaced by the arrival of his younger brothers. 'Father' is written in narrow lettering from which can be inferred the source of Freddy's inhibitions and frustrations. But all is not well in his relationship with his mother either, for that word is corrected. As for the word 'kitchen' (final word, bottom line), he actually stammers when writing it, for he starts it three times before he succeeds in writing it. Some most unpleasant situations seem to have arisen in this room or to be connected with it.

Freddy has sketched the penknife cleverly. The drawing shows manual dexterity. Having been promoted to the possession of a knife, the boy sees it as an important object. It marks a definite advance in his life. Toys have ceased to arouse interest, but a penknife is an adult's possession. The first penknife usually shows the line of demarcation between childhood and puberty, and it is interesting to see Freddy's regard for his.

In spite of a progressive and unconventional upbringing, Freddy shows many alternating symptoms of tension and release. We have to find out how to overcome the tension, conquer the repressions that impede his rhythm and help him to attain happiness. A somewhat labile mentality does not create placid behaviour and, if we take Freddy's impressionability into account also, we cannot expect the boy to be even-tempered. In calm moods he is simple and unassuming, but in an exalted state of mind he can be very trying.

Freddy is endowed with a good brain and he likes to show off. He is used to impressing his elders and to being admired. His many interests are not due merely to a thirst for knowledge; a great deal of curiosity is at play and he likes to pry into affairs that should not concern him yet.

The boy seems to be at war with the concept 'truth'. He does not deliberately tell a lie, but he is extremely subtle in bridging awkward situations. This quality in his character needs careful watching. What causes an evasion of truth: is it frustration, fear or insecurity? Does his schooling come into the matter and can his evasion of truth result from educational mistakes? It may be due to an anti-parental attitude or it may be a reaction to a strict discipline at school. It is most important to find out the reason. Freddy needs emotional release; punishment would only intensify the conflict.

Although he has grown up with two brothers, the boy feels lonely; in fact he seems to prefer solitude which is unusual. It is significant that he gets spasms of depression in spite of an innate optimism.

Psychologically well-trained people should be entrusted with solving Freddy's difficulties. He needs the maximum help with the minimum interference. This can best be obtained at a Child Guidance Clinic. His potentialities will offer him a wide choice of career, which can be decided on when it is seen how his development proceeds.

This handwriting analysis was followed by a second ten months later. Figure 28 gives the second sample of writing and this is the report on it:

The letter started with under-emphasis and it was only towards the end of it that Freddy mustered more courage.

The word 'Mummy' is again corrected, though 'Daddy' is spelt with capital letters revealing an admiring attitude towards the father. The drawing is expressive and well explained.

A certain measure of improvement can be detected, but the main conflicts are not completely solved, in spite of the fact that the parents have done their best to help the boy to understand himself. While fear and anxiety have decreased, reticence and concealment can still be noted. In fact some parts of the boy's handwriting betray regression. He still needs skilled help.

FIG. 28

The next case concerns Philip who is aged 11 and whose writing can be seen in Figures 29, 30 and 31. The report on his handwriting was as follows:

Philip is a very likeable and intelligent boy who is more mature than his chronological age.

His logical and clear way of thinking is combined with a marked critical faculty, but he is highly-strung, tense and excitable and this condition causes nervous disturbances and emotional stress. Although quick in the uptake he is slow in response, his rhythm

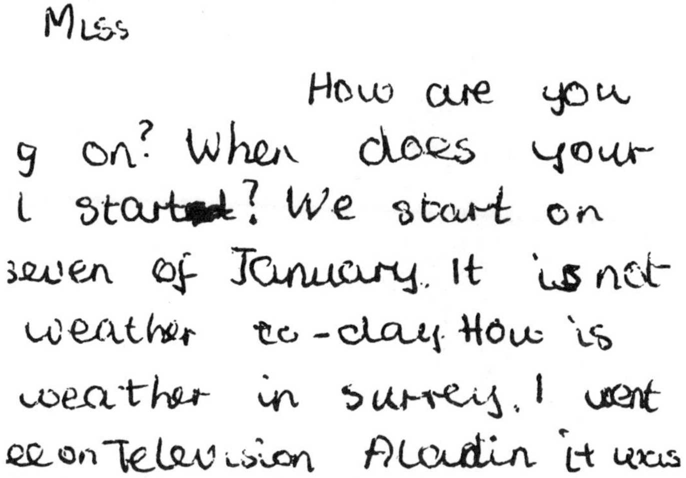

Miss

How are you
g on? When does your
l startod? We start on
seven of January. It is not
weather to-day How is
weather in surrey. I went
ee on Television Aladin it was

FIG. 29

being retarded by panic and exaggerated prudence. Philip cannot 'take things easy' but is obsessionally painstaking. He dare not come to the fore because he fears defeat, but sometimes he will over-compensate for this by being foolhardy or bumptious.

This disturbed rhythm caused by emotional maladjustment can be observed in his handwriting quite easily. He is obviously trying hard to control his excitability but this only causes more tension. He is not moody in the ordinary sense of the words; his imbalance is due to an inadequate outlet for his overstressed emotions.

The slip of paper, Figure 30, was written in an exalted frame of mind, and the words, 'Philip is mad today' lead to the inference that the boy recognizes his own lack of balance.

Philip is by no means anti-social but he does find it difficult to form attachments. He could love and be lovable were it not for his nervous fear. New experiences and new surroundings frighten him so much that he suffers severe psychological upsets whenever he is confronted with a change.

The drawing of the teddy bear in Figure 31 was produced in a

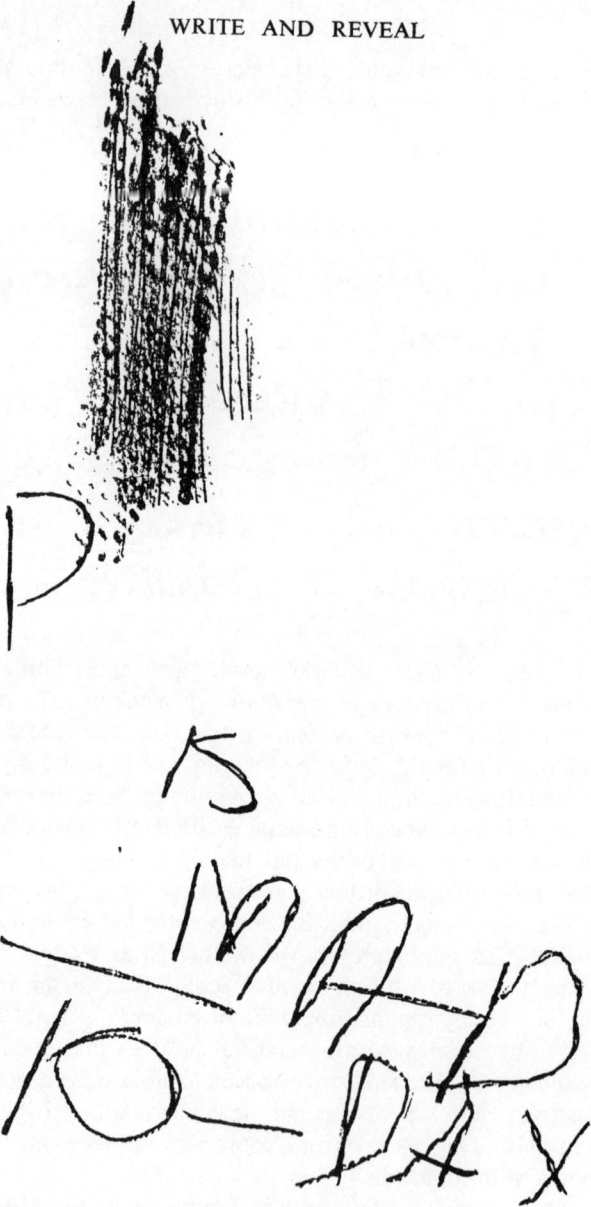

FIG. 30

bout of high spirits which frequently alternate with a morbid state
of mind. A good sense of form, space and proportion is expressed

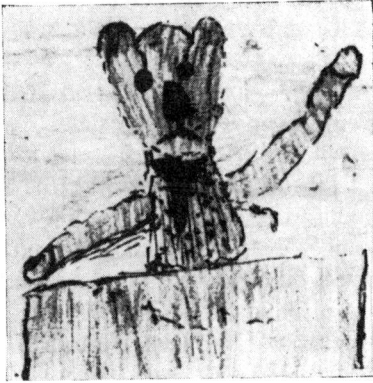

FIG. 31 (reduced)

in this drawing, and this is a very encouraging symptom. Although
Philip is not likely to turn to art as his profession, drawing and
painting will always form a satisfying hobby for him.

Many phases of development and new facets of his personality
will have to come under review before a profession can be chosen
for him. Any pursuit, however, which needs sound reasoning,
observation of detail and skill in figures would be suitable for him.
Accountancy, psychometrics, economics or statistics should be
open to him provided his nervous instability improves.

His development from puberty to adolescence may bring surprises both pleasant and unpleasant, but this will not be unexpected
in view of his precarious psychological structure.

The report ends there, but Philip's case-history is such a clear
example of what a broken home can do to a boy that it is given
here also.

Philip's parents emigrated from Germany to England in 1939.
The father, then nineteen years old, came of a wealthy family; the
mother, who was eighteen, was an only and spoilt child of middle-
class background. The father took up tool-making in England and
is now skilled in his work. Philip was born in 1941 and was the

second child. Soon after his birth the parents separated, Philip remaining with his mother while the father claimed the elder boy. The parents' separation was followed by a divorce. The father disassociated himself completely from Philip who was placed in a residential nursery till his fourth year. He was then boarded out and suffered severe deprivations. There is no doubt that these sad experiences coloured his life to a large extent.

At the age of seven Philip entered a hostel for displaced children. Here he was a general favourite of wardens and children. But the damage had been done. Philip dislikes his mother and she has no affection for him. He does not know his father. His nervous condition is the direct outcome of a broken home and the experiences in which it involved a small child.

The next case is that of Eva, aged fourteen, whose writing can be seen in Figures 32, 33 and 34.

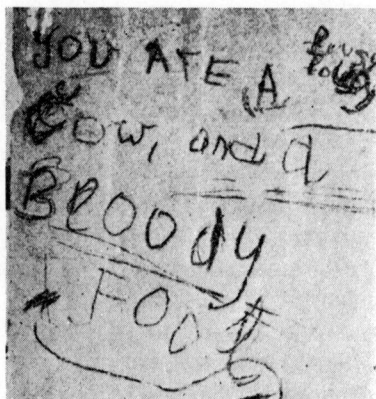

FIG. 32 (reduced)

The head mistress of a well-known girls' school was at a loss to account for destructive actions in the cloakroom. The coats of some girls were slit with a sharp instrument and at the same time anonymous notes, drawn in coloured crayons and couched in abusive language, were left in the coat pockets. The notes read as follows: Note 1 (Figure 32) 'You are a lousy cow and a bloody fool.'

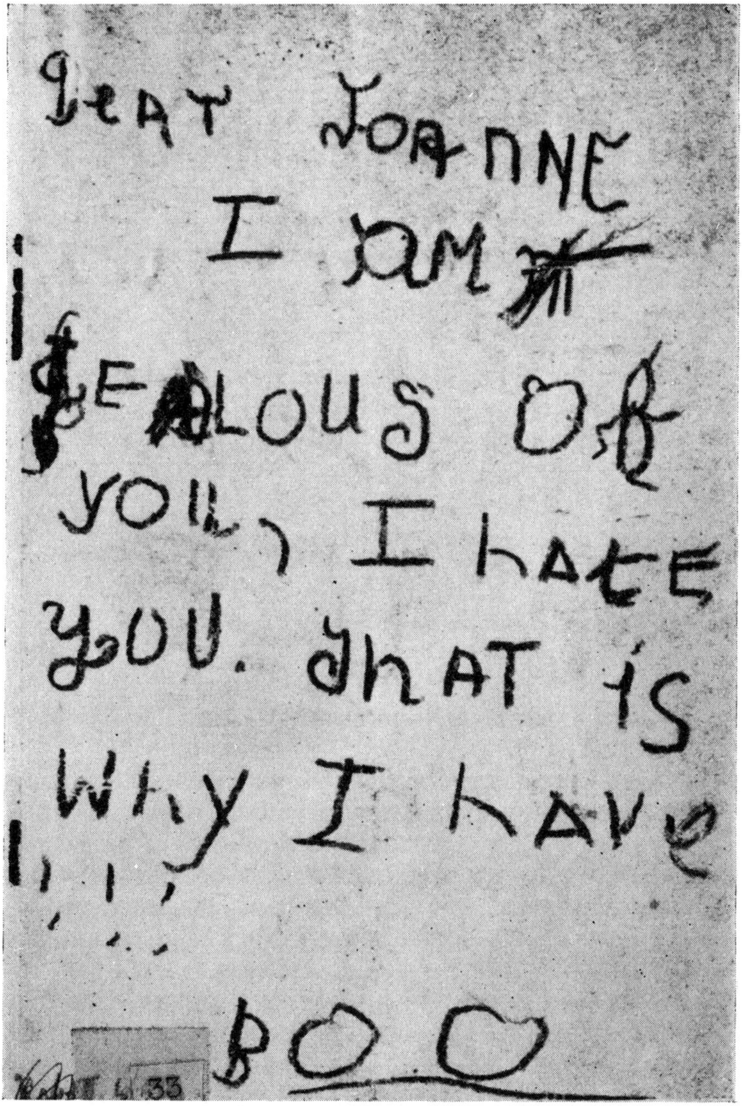

dEAr JoAnne
I am
jEALOUS of
you, I hAtE
you. thAT is
why I have

BOO

FIG. 33

Note 2 (Figure 33) 'Dear Joanne, I am jealous of you, I hate you, that is why I have!!! signed 'Boo.'

The task was to identify the culprit. Only two or three specimens of the handwriting of the suspects were available (Figures 34 and 35). The similarities between these and the coloured notes were not fully convincing. More incriminating material was needed to supplement this scanty evidence before the problem could be solved with certainty. The head mistress therefore helped the graphologist to get this evidence by dictating to the upper forms of the school a skilfully made-up fable in which the stimulus-words were embedded.

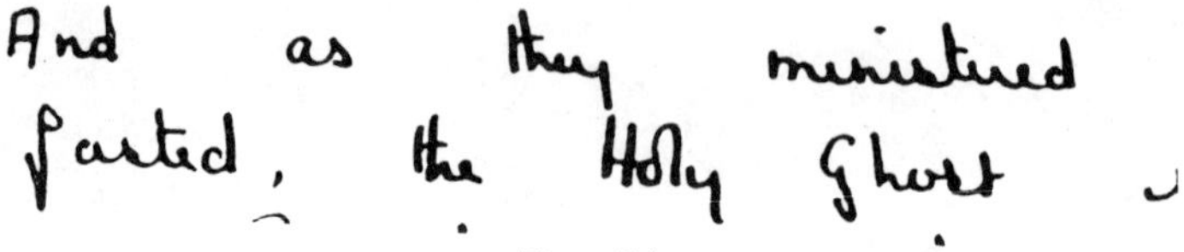

FIG. 34

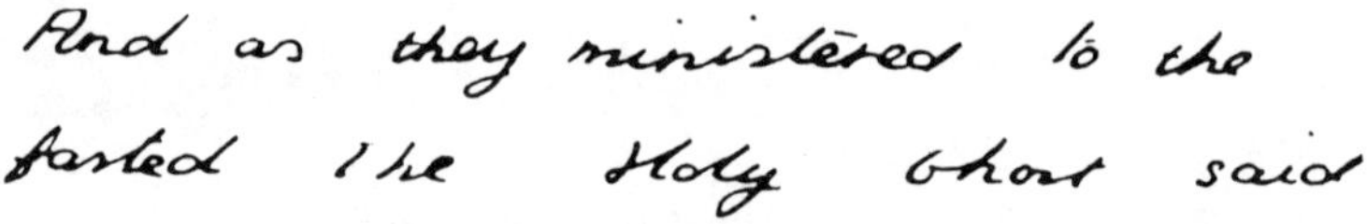

FIG. 35

The dictation figures are numbers 36, 37, 38 and 39. The text of the fable was as follows:

'The grasshopper sighed as from his perch on the clover flowers he surveyed the *cow* standing knee-deep in the stream.

"How cool she must be on this hot summer day," he muttered, temporarily ceasing to sing, "and how I wish I could change places with her." The wood-*louse* that clung sleeping at the bottom of a nearby stone heard him and awoke. "My *dear* grasshopper," he said, "to be *jealous* of the *cow* is to show yourself a *fool*. How would *you* like to spend the whole of this long summer day energetically flicking your tail to keep off the flies who would feed on your very *blood*?" "Why of course I should *hate* it," said the grasshopper, feeling rather ashamed of his grumbling, "but I never thought of it in this way." "Just learn to think another time before you give way to envy and wake other people up with your lamentations," said the *louse* curling himself up into a little scaly ball, and although the grasshopper had a rhetorical peroration ready, his mentor was asleep before he could utter it.'

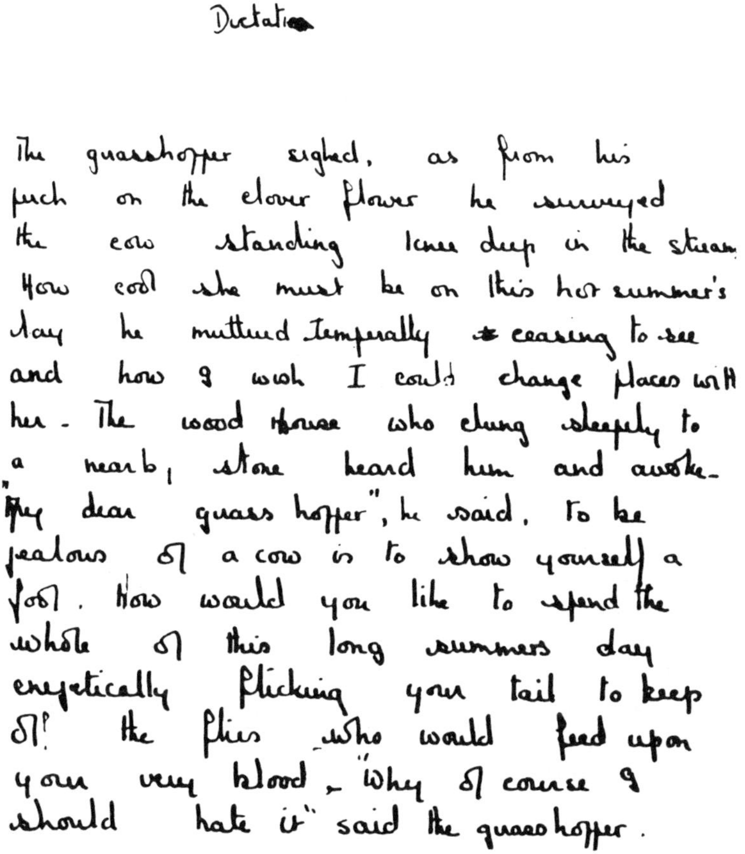

Dictation

The grasshopper sighed, as from his perch on the clover flower he surveyed the cow standing knee deep in the stream. How cool she must be on this hot summer's day he muttered Temporally & ceasing to see and how I wish I could change places with her. The wood house who clung sleepily to a nearby stone heard him and awoke. "My dear grasshopper", he said, To be jealous of a cow is to show yourself a fool. How would you like to spend the whole of this long summers day energetically flicking your tail to keep off the flies who would feed upon your very blood. Why of course I should hate it" said the grasshopper.

FIG. 36 (reduced)

The emotion betrayed in the stimulus-words italicized above when written by Eva (Figures 36 and 37), who had been suspected in the first place, left no doubt that she had actually written those notes. The word *wood-louse* (line 7, Figure 36) is shaky and corrected, thus betraying an emotional strain. *Louse* (line 5, Figure 37) is also corrected. The words *jealous* and *fool* have sudden strong angles in the j and in the f, (lines 10 and 11, Figure 36), which indicate an aggression absent from Eva's usual style of writing. The whole dictation is written constrainedly and shows intense inhibition and a feeling of guilt.

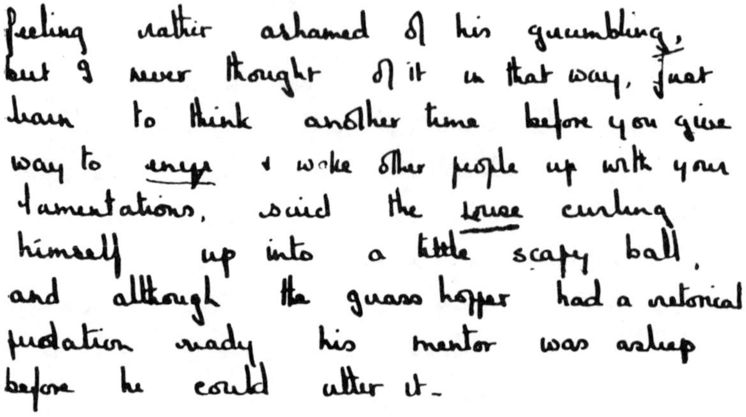

feeling rather ashamed of his grumbling, but I never thought of it in that way, just learn to think another time before you give way to anger & woke other people up with your lamentations, said the louse curling himself up into a little scary ball, and although the grass hopper had a rhetorical peroration ready his mentor was asleep before he could utter it —

FIG. 37 (reduced)

The head mistress who was well-versed in psychology, took the graphologist's advice and befriended Eva who was badly in need of affection and understanding.

Eva's best friend, Alice, also showed symptoms of emotion in the stimulus-words in her dictation (Figures 38 and 39). The trembling strokes and the corrections can be seen in Figure 38. Look at *cow* (line 2), *louse* (line 7) and *you,* written as *yeu* (line 11). Apprehension is obvious in the word *louse* (line 5, Figure 39). The sentiments betrayed in these significant words are proof that Eva's best friend was 'in the know', so the evidence of the two girls' handwritings brought the matter to a clear conclusion. We knew who had done the deeds: it remained to find out why she had done them.

Eva's relationship with a harsh mother was determined from graphological symptoms. The psychological conclusion was evident. As Eva could not succeed in acquiring attention by fair means she

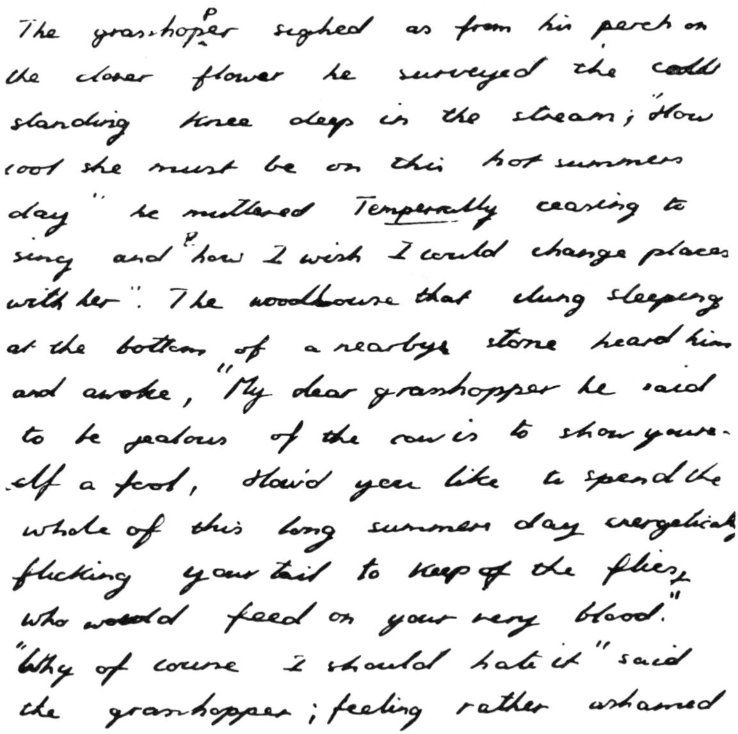

The grasshopper sighed as from his perch on
the clover flower he surveyed the cow
standing knee deep in the stream; "How
cool she must be on this hot summer's
day" he muttered Temperally ceasing to
sing and "how I wish I could change places
with her". The woodlouse that clung sleeping
at the bottom of a nearby stone heard him
and awoke, "My dear grasshopper he said
to be jealous of the cow is to show yourself a fool, How'd you like to spend the
whole of this long summer's day energetically
flicking your tail to keep off the flies,
who would feed on your very blood."
"Why of course I should hate it" said
the grasshopper; feeling rather ashamed

FIG. 38 (reduced)

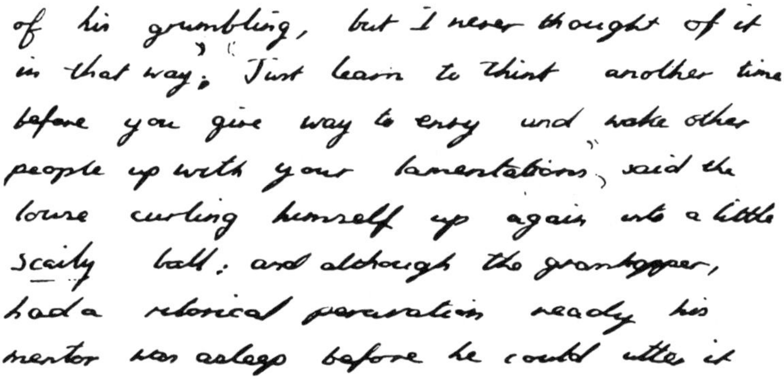

of his grumbling, but I never thought of it
in that way." Just learn to think another time
before you give way to envy and wake other
people up with your lamentations," said the
louse curling himself up again into a little
scaly ball; and although the grasshopper,
had a rhetorical peroration ready his
mentor was asleep before he could utter it

FIG. 39 (reduced)

resorted to foul. She could not risk giving vent to outbreaks of revenge at home, and, being convinced that nobody at school would suspect the fact that she, a well-mannered girl of a refined background, would play such tricks, she carried them out there.

The next case concerns Norah, aged 14, whose writing can be seen in Figure 40.

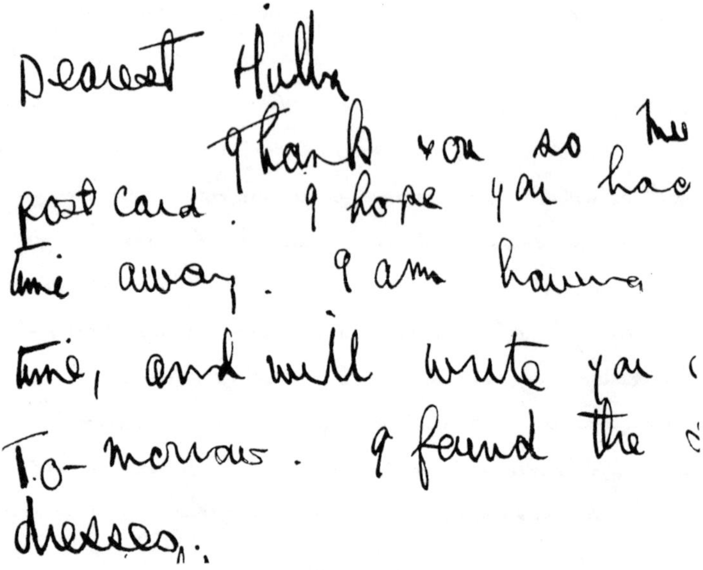
Dearest Hilda
Thank you so
post card. I hope you had
time away. I am having
time, and will write you
To-morrow. I found the
dresses.

FIG. 40

The writer is without doubt a difficult child to handle, for she insists on having her own way but will not take the trouble to explain her point of view. We are emphatically confronted with a person in all the difficulties of puberty. Norah has been a problem-child from nursery days and has always shown a marked maladjustment to life. Now she is physically over-developed, but quite unprepared for the demands of sexual maturity. She is in fact incapable of coping with the perplexities of her condition, and the dynamic forces at work in her often take an unpleasant form and lead to tantrums, erratic moods, depression and general discontent.

It seems as if the strife between Norah's parents is showing repercussions in the child. Her emotional balance is so upset that her behaviour is completely incomprehensible to those surrounding her. By preference she isolates herself in order to indulge in morbid imaginings and hypochondriac trends of thought. She is very secretive and tries to hide her feelings. She therefore resents interference and is reluctant to let anybody look into her affairs. She worries unduly over humiliating experiences and, being hypersensitive, her feelings are easily hurt.

Norah has always been a centre of attention and wants to be admired so she sometimes gives vent to self-display. She is irritated when she is considered a child and therefore compensates herself with a pronounced feeling of self-esteem. She cannot concentrate on any sort of work for she lacks the power of concentration. It is of the utmost importance to rouse her to some form of activity, no matter what, in order to banish her lethargy.

This girl is not bad; in fact at times she is seriously disgusted with her own shortcomings. Only gentle guidance and a full understanding of her mentality can lead to positive results. The time for vocational guidance will not be ripe until her difficulties and defiance are overcome. Psychological treatment could in all probability direct her wilfulness into more useful channels and at the same time speed up her rhythm.

John, our next case, is aged 15. His writing can be seen in Figure 41. A handwriting analysis was required to determine whether he is a potential delinquent or a potential neurotic. This is the report on him:

John's writing shows that he is a very sensitive, highly-strung youth. He is a considerate boy, always anxious to please, for he likes to be considered a general favourite. He does not believe in his own potentialities and feels insecure. So he likes to adhere to a pattern and does not dare to be original. Although he is of good average intelligence he has a slow rhythm. John is a perseverator and therefore cannot switch over quickly from impression to expression.

It is of paramount importance to guard this boy from uncongenial associates, for he is egocentric, weak-willed and vacillating, and his resistance to external influences is insufficient. He is concealing, secretive and not altogether truthful. He likes to pretend and is moody and capricious, character-traits that are often seen in a weak personality.

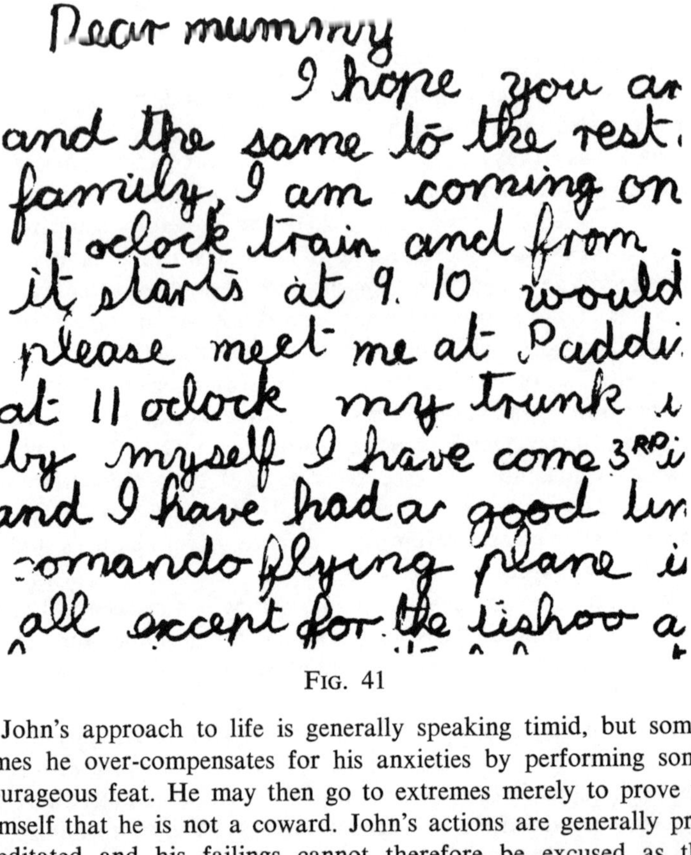

Dear mummy
I hope you ar
and the same to the rest,
family, I am coming on
11 oclock train and from.
it starts at 9. 10 would
please meet me at Paddi.
at 11 oclock my trunk i
by myself I have come 3rd i
and I have had a good lev
comando flying plane i
all except for the lishoo a

FIG. 41

John's approach to life is generally speaking timid, but sometimes he over-compensates for his anxieties by performing some courageous feat. He may then go to extremes merely to prove to himself that he is not a coward. John's actions are generally premeditated and his failings cannot therefore be excused as the outcome of momentary provocation which would be less harmful.

Frustration in early childhood seems to be responsible for this boy's severe tension. We see him as a cramped individual superimposing an external composure on his pent-up emotions which clamour for release. The boy is in need of help in his difficulty but must be allowed to work out his own salvation. The main conflict lies in the inner circle of family relationships. His attitude to his mother is particularly ambivalent. Her influence is too overbearing. Being dominated by a strong personality increases John's tension, so that he appears to be in revolt against all authority. Too much care is bestowed on the boy and not enough love. Although he likes a firm guiding hand for the sake of security, he resents being regimented. Lavish and undivided love and full appreciation of his attempts are likely to bring out the best in him and at the same time restore his self-confidence. He needs self-respect. The strong feeling of guilt that he has and that is part of his neurotic character can be overcome by only one remedy, forgiveness. Patience must be exercised in his home, where without expert assistance he could be helped to better self-adjustment. In bringing the positive aspects of his nature to the fore his family could help him towards fuller maturity.

John feels very lonely and being a-social he has no affection for his fellowbeings. He must learn to accept himself in spite of his weaknesses. As soon as his faith in himself is restored his abilities are likely to unfold. Approval and a warm relationship within the family should help towards fuller integration of his personality. He cannot at present give free rein to his potentialities because he is in the throes of a serious neurosis.

Several specimens of John's writing were examined and, according to graphological symptoms which are not all shown in the small sample of writing given here, the verdict on John is that he is not a potential delinquent but that he is a trying neurotic.

CHAPTER FIVE

Vocational Guidance

Graphology is of great use in guiding young people in the choice of a career and it should always be allied to the usual vocational tests. Adolescents, generally speaking, are incapable of knowing which career is most suitable to their make-up and only a very few of them feel a strong urge for a certain profession. Even those few may be mistaken for, although the inclination to one particular career may be strong, their greatest potentialities may lie in another direction. The person who can best help the young adolescent to find the path he should follow is he who has the ability to see beyond the conscious level. Parents are not the best people to advise their children in this matter. Too often they wish to see their own unfulfilled ambitions realised by their offspring and therefore direct their children towards a career that they themselves were denied. Occasionally, contrariwise, they force their children to take over a business that they have successfully built up or to follow a profession where their own experience might be a useful asset. This way of choosing a career regardless of the child's capabilities, intelligence and disposition can result only in unhappiness for the individual and loss to the community. The safest way to determine the road the adolescent should take is to seek the advice of the psychologist and the graphologist.

Here is the first vocational guidance report. It concerns Paul, aged 16, whose writing can be seen in Figure 42.

Paul is a man in the making who has attained a high ethical standard and excellent self-discipline. It is unusual for a boy of his age to show already a set character, but Paul is able to discriminate between right and wrong with sound judgment in a manner worthy of a well-balanced adult. He is energetic, persistent and determined, but at the same time cautious, timid and hesitating. By nature he is quick, excitable and of a nervous disposition, but his sense of responsibility makes him halt and thus prevents him from overshooting the mark.

Though quick-tempered and vivacious he has himself well in

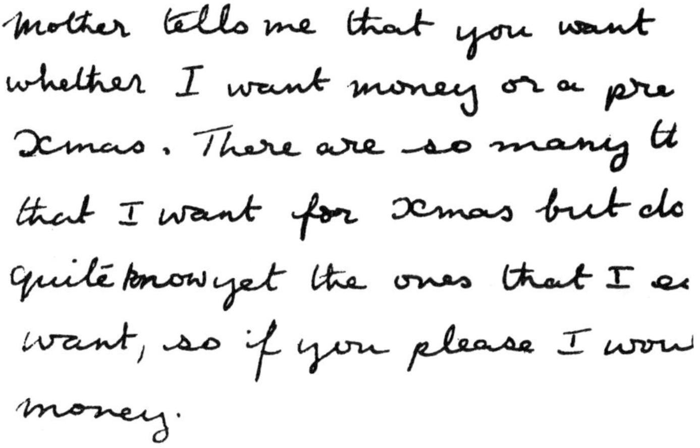

Mother tells me that you want whether I want money or a pre Xmas. There are so many tt that I want for Xmas but do quite know yet the ones that I ei want, so if you please I wou money.

FIG. 42

hand by means of this self-discipline. He carefully ponders over the pros and cons of a situation with the result that reason conquers impulse with a self-restraint rare in young people.

Paul is a staunch friend, frank, truthful and outspoken without being demonstrative. Being of a lovable and sympathetic disposition he makes friends easily. In short he is a chivalrous youth of inborn nobility.

A modern upbringing helped Paul to grow up without inhibitions. All the same there is apparent that hesitant manner frequently found in Public School boys, which is due to the fear of making oneself conspicuous in some way. This apprehension impedes Paul's spontaneity to a certain extent.

Love of detail, clear and precise thinking, objective judgment and a fertile intelligence give this boy full scope to choose a congenial vocation. It is quite evident that he is predestined for an academic career.

Graphologists occasionally hear later news of the adolescents whose writing is sent to them. Paul became a doctor and is now well-established as a medical practitioner in a provincial town.

The next report concerns Andrew, also aged 16, whose writing can be seen in Figures 43 and 44.

71

Even an untrained eye can see the difference between these two samples of Andrew's writing. The narrow writing, strong pressure

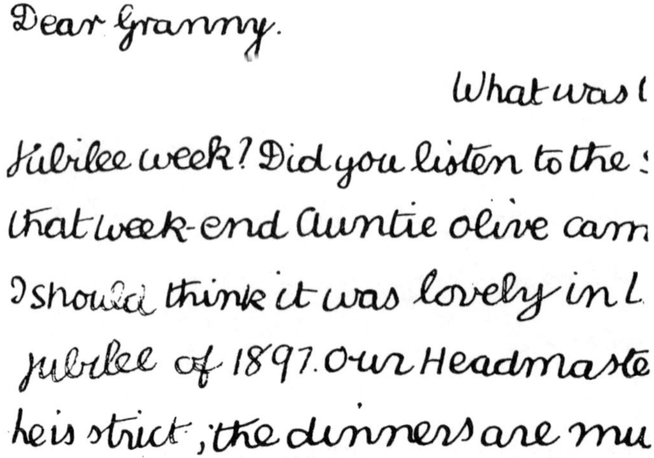

Dear Granny.

What was [

Jubilee week? Did you listen to the ?

that week-end Auntie olive cam

I should think it was lovely in L

jubilee of 1897. Our Headmaste

he is strict, the dinners are mu

FIG. 43

and general rigidity of Figure 43 which is addressed to Andrew's Granny shows mental retardation. Figure 44 which is addressed to his Aunt is produced with more ease. A comparsion of the two specimens thus provides an indication that there is a source of conflict and where it can be found. If more evidence were needed we have only to look at Figure 44, which is written with less heavy pressure and is wider and generally fluent, and in which the only outstanding word is *Granny* in line 6. Without doubt that word is the clue to Andrew's difficulties.

This boy is unable to work and his inability is due to an emotional upheaval. He seems to be vibrating underneath his external composure which is kept with intense self-control, thus wasting part of his energy and detracting from the quality of his work. In many ways Andrew is a clever boy. He has a particular gift for drawing. His innate abilities are superior to his acquired knowledge. Regression seems to have taken place and the boy has turned neurotic. Owing to his nervous disposition he must be approached step by step. He is in need of encouragement, recognition and freedom to

72

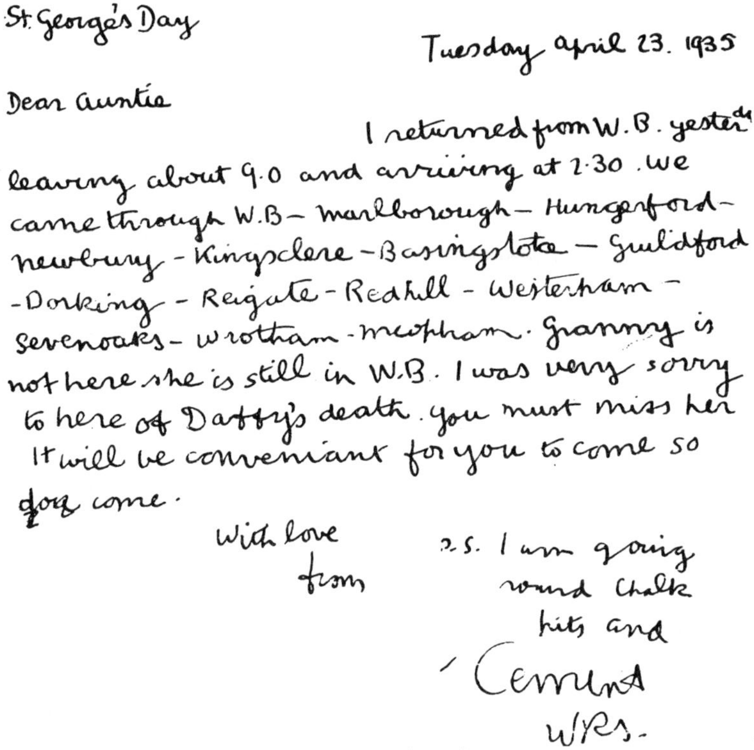

St. George's Day

Tuesday April 23. 1935

Dear Auntie

I returned from W.B. yesterᵈ leaving about 9.0 and arriving at 2.30. We came through W.B — Marlborough — Hungerford — newbury — Kingsclere — Basingstoke — Guildford — Dorking — Reigate — Redhill — Westerham — Sevenoaks — Wrotham — Meopham. Granny is not here she is still in W.B. I was very sorry to here of Daffy's death. you must miss her It will be conveniant for you to come so dog come.

With love
from

P.S. I am going round Chalk pits and

Cement
W/Rs.

FIG. 44 (reduced)

reorganize his life according to his own needs. He should be helped in his development and not forced into it, and suitable means of self-expression should be found to liberate his repressed energy.

Andrew's handwriting shows that his career can best be chosen in draughtsmanship or architecture, and it would be wise to guide his creative and constructive abilities gently towards the easiest approach to such usefulness. As soon as the difficulties in his relationship with his Granny have been overcome he may do well as a builder or an architect. It is obvious that behind the problem child are the problem parents, but in this case it is the problem grandmother who has to take the blame.

The report ended there, but when the full details of the boy's state of mind and directions as to the method of improving it were reported to the parents and the grandmother, the atmosphere was soon cleared. Graphologists do not often get the chance to know whether their advice has been followed and if it has borne fruit. In this case, however, we heard that Andrew had made good progress at school and had made up his mind to pass the entrance examination at an architectural college.

Another 16-year-old is Nicholas, whose writing can be seen in Figures 45 and 46.

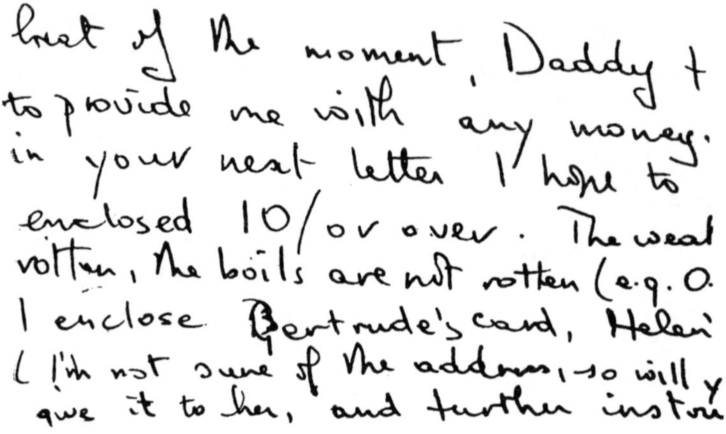

brat of the moment, Daddy +
to provide me with any money.
in your next letter I hope to
enclosed 10/or over. The weal
rotten, the boils are not rotten (e.g. O.
I enclose Bertrude's card, Helen
(I'm not sure of the address, so will y
gue it to her, and further instru

FIG. 45

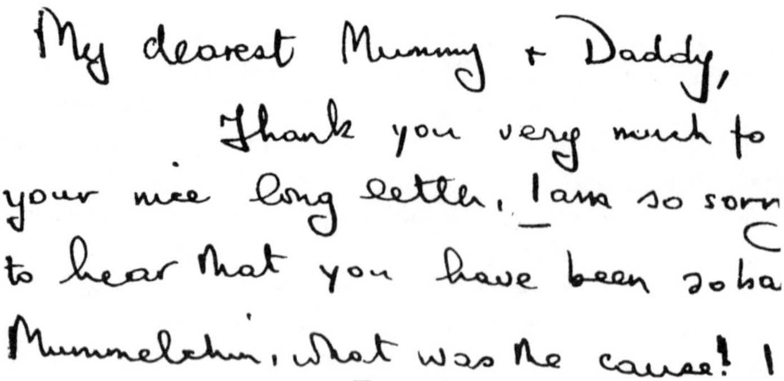

My dearest Mummy + Daddy,
Thank you very much to
your nice long letter, I am so sorn
to hear that you have been so ha
Mummelchin, what was the cause! I

FIG. 46

The restlessness and unsettled state common at his age are clearly expressed in Nicholas' handwriting. He has a long way to go before he is truly adult. In some ways he is already surprisingly advanced, but in others he is much younger than his chronological age. This in itself constitutes a conflict, the man in him driving him to advanced achievements while the child holds him back so that he often regresses into infantile behaviour.

At times Nicholas can work out his problems with logic. His mind is active and well-developed, and his vivacity, when not given too free a rein, is stimulating. His potentialities are manifold, so that good prospects lie ahead for him, but at present he is lazy and easy-going so that he is not likely to do great things just yet. It is not wise to harp on his failings, for he is fully aware of them. He needs encouragement more than upbraiding.

Nicholas is fond of reading and appreciative of literature for he has a receptive mind. In spite of a large measure of common sense and a practical mind, he has a lively imagination which can carry him away so that sometimes his fantasies are apt to become realities to him. He is fond of controversy and arguments, and his brilliant discussions have a quality of bold directness quite amazing at times. Perhaps he is too blunt and outspoken to be appreciated by others, especially as his frankness is mostly a disguised form of aggression.

Nicholas is inconsistent in every respect; he is reserved, secretive and modest, and yet at times strikingly ostentatious. He rarely forms a balanced judgment about himself but either over-rates or under-rates his abilities.

This boy is easily fatigued and even exhausted. In comparing himself with stronger boys he often revolts against this physical weakness and a pretended manliness then serves as a cloak for the disadvantages caused by his delicate constitution.

His father seems to play an important part in his life and Nicholas tries to find security by leaning on him. His feelings towards his mother are ambivalent, i.e. partly affectionate and partly resentful. He prefers to act as her protector.

Nicholas's intellectual interests are genuine, but his inertia tips the scale against worth-while achievements. A commercial sense and a practical mind are emphasized, so that he would be well-advised to follow a business career in preference to academic studies. He is fond of money and interested in material gains, tendencies which can be more easily satisfied in the commercial than in the professional world.

Figures 47 and 48/49 show the writing of Leonie, aged 16, and of David, her brother, aged 18.

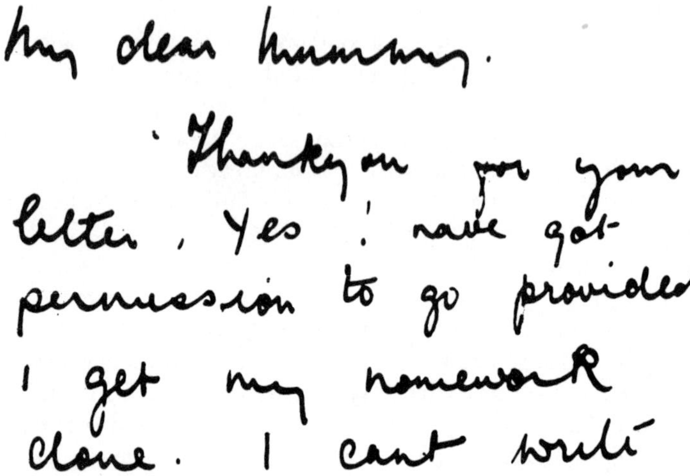
My dear Mummy.
Thank you for your letter, Yes I have got permission to go provided I get my homework done. I cant write

FIG. 47

Leonie's writing shows that she is a very sensitive girl whose overactive mind feels a strong need to express itself. She is of high intelligence and gifted in many ways. She is quite aware of her superiority over the average sort of person and is not patient with the shortcomings of others. She is, in fact, rather apt to under-rate their achievements.

Affectionate, open, pleasant and straight, Leonie is a very likeable girl, but being hypersensitive she reacts to the slightest vibration in her surroundings. At present she tends to indulge a morbid state of mind, is dreamy, absent-minded and sometimes involved in a vague state of fear. Her aggressive moods often take the form of sudden bursts of temper.

In spite of her general ease of manner, Leonie easily gets depressed and makes an undue burden of her life, worrying more than is justified by circumstances. This morbid trend is often experienced during adolescence, but it is a phase likely to disappear once a choice of future career is settled. Any sort of academic or literary work would be within this girl's scope. She also has artistic inclinations, good taste and a facile and quick way of expressing herself in an easy flow of language. Her mental vivacity leaves many avenues open to her for a profession. Journalism or librarianship might be suggested, as as an alternative, a position as private secretary to a writer or diplomat. On attaining full womanhood much of her pessimism is likely to fade away.

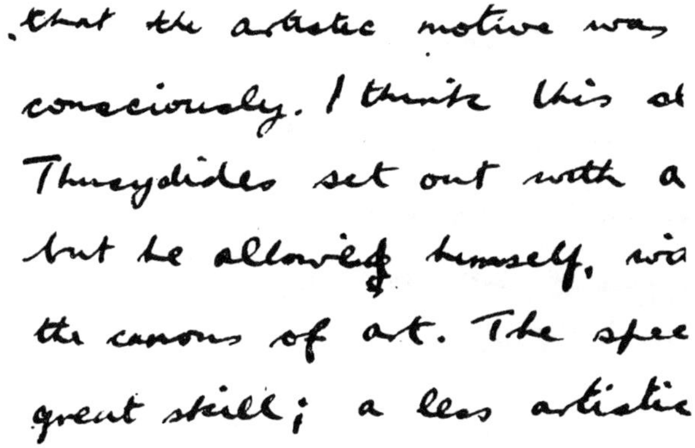

FIG. 48

From all the material sent for analysis, handwriting specimens from his fourteenth to eighteenth year, it is evident that David showed a set character at a comparatively early age. He was rather precocious, had a clear idea of the way in which he wished to shape his life and was never enthusiastic about taking the advice of others.

On the intellectual level the boy has succeeded to a considerable extent for he is able to use discrimination in his judgment and to follow his road with tenacity and yet with flexibility. He is progressive in outlook which stands him in good stead. By nature he is extremely kind, conciliatory and patient and he does not shirk responsibilities. He has a keen awareness of his limitations; in fact an exaggerated idea of the inadequacies of his character causes him undue anxiety. It is not easy for him to tame his impetuosity, and it takes him by surprise that in spite of severe self-discipline unconscious wishes come to the fore and create difficulties.

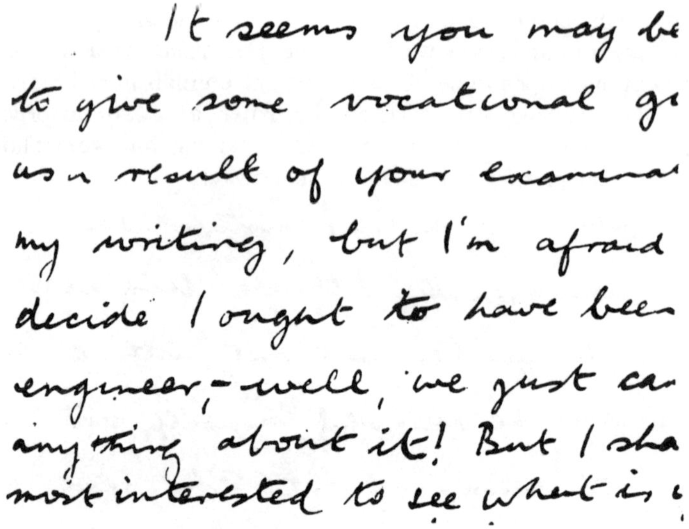

It seems you may be to give some vocational gu as a result of your examina my writing, but I'm afraid decide I ought to have bee engineer, — well, we just ca anything about it! But I sha most interested to see what is

FIG. 49

David rarely yields to impressions without checking them intellectually. Being a classics scholar should form a firm basis for his future profession. He is a born teacher, for he has not only a lucid way of interpreting and imparting knowledge to others but also the ability to understand their psychological make-up. This facile empathy is an asset for a teacher, but an additional and comprehensive study of psychology would enhance David's chances.

The principal dissonance in his character is due to his relationship with his parents. There is a great family likeness between mother and son, as can be observed in a letter from his mother (Figure 50). But David has the urge to detach himself from his mother's protection while at the same time trying to avoid hurting her feelings. The mother, however, is not prepared to give up her role of protector which she considers her right. David tries to identify himself with his father, but this in turn prevents him from developing his own personality to its full extent and inhibits the possibility of testing his own powers. This situation naturally creates conflict. A temporary change of surroundings would probably alleviate the tension.

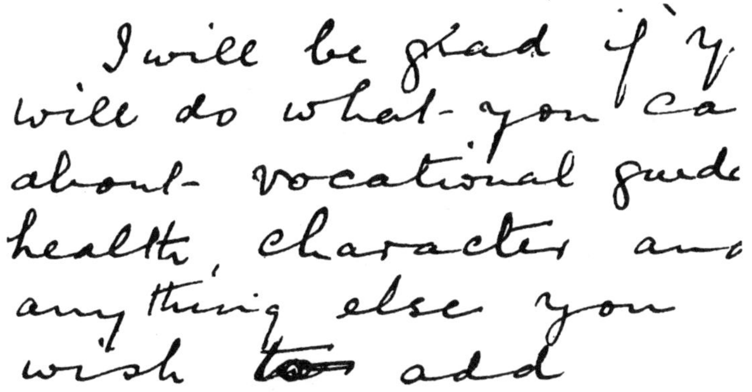

FIG. 50

David is not constitutionally robust, a fact that makes him feel at a disadvantage. He is not fond of sport and having neglected this side of his development he needs a certain amount of organized leisure to counterbalance his sedentary work. To enable him to obtain the full advantage of his potentialities the accent should now be slightly shifted from occupations of the intellect to those of the body. Plenty of fresh air and some sport or gymnastics would improve his circulation and help him in every way to develop more freely.

The next case concerns Ethel who is aged 18 and whose writing can be seen in Figure 51.

Ethel's charm lies in her great kindness and naturalness and in her love of nature to which she feels closely drawn. Her motto, without any sort of pretence, is; Here I am, take me as you find me. One might be able to interpret this attitude as arrogant in some people, but Ethel is of a retiring gentle temperament, a girl who tries to avoid controversy and friction and to enjoy the simple pleasures of life. Externalities do not play an important part in her life and she does not cultivate any sort of vanity.

In Ethel spontaneity and indecision alternate and a mixture of courage and insecurity sets up an inner conflict. This irregular flow of her energy seems to be due to physiological conditions affecting her emotional level.

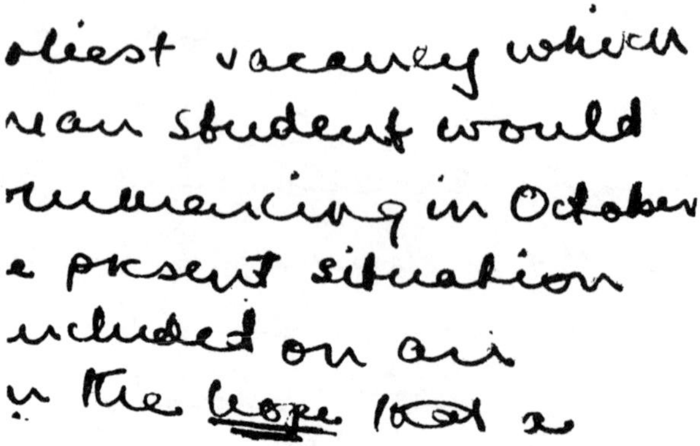

FIG. 51

In many ways Ethel is original and she has a certain naive confidence in herself, and yet in other ways she shows great psychic dependence and is thus inclined to absorb too readily the influence of those surrounding her. She imitates the people who appeal to her without exercising the necessary criticism. Although in need of affection and friendship she does not easily make social contacts. Pessimistic thoughts and a certain measure of distrust of her fellows complicate her social adaptation. Her emotions are over-emphasized and being aware of these exaggerated feelings she is hard at work to repress them.

Ethel is somewhat playful, particularly in regard to work. She needs a more regular output of energy to achieve good results. Work interests her only to while away the time, and more for the sake of recreation than for the sake of achievement. Mainsprings of energy, such as ambition or vanity, are completely lacking in her mentality and having to choose a career alarms her because she does not like to organize her abilities for material gain.

Ethel tries to appear nonchalant, using this attitude as a defence-mechanism; but she is not nearly as emancipated as she appears to be. She can be curt and unmindful of criticism and yet at the same time waste her energy in trying to adapt herself to a conventional pattern. In some ways she shows a carefree, even careless attitude, but in others she is over-conscientious and highly-principled. She dissects and analyzes her thoughts and actions too much for she is far too introspective. In this way small details become important worries in her mind. In spite of all her difficulties, however, she keeps a sane balance in her world of ever-changing impulses, emotions and dislikes.

To satisfy her nature, of which Ethel is probably not conscious, she ought at least for a time to engage in some sort of agricultural work. It would not only improve her physical condition and gratify her love of nature, but it would at the same time provide an outlet for her repressions. Sedentary work cannot achieve the main object, which is to set her going. When once she is fully mature, for at present she is troubled with the complexities of a delayed puberty, she may attain the security which she needs.

Our last case concerns Charles, aged 19, whose writing can be seen in Fig. 52, 52a and 52b.

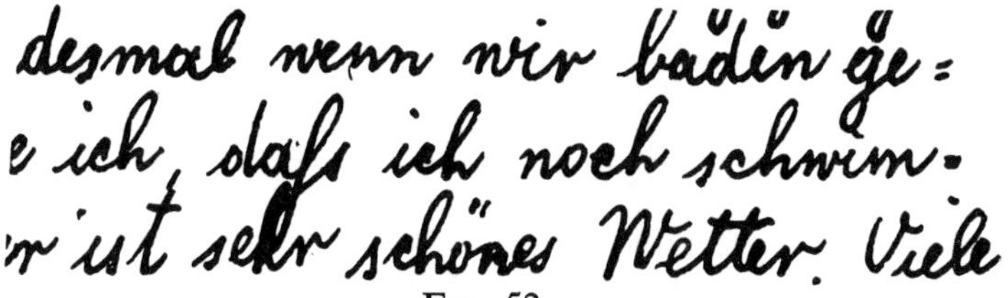

FIG. 52

This is the writing of a very sensitive young man. According to his chronological age he should have full adolescence, but owing to a maladjustment a regression has taken place. Several scripts were available for examination and they showed that at the age of puberty Fig. 52 and 52a, Charles's development was promising. He was in fact precocious. At that time he was a natural and simple boy, whereas in his later scripts he shows that he is unduly involved and artificial. His rhythm and his movements have changed. In Fig.

52 he was eleven years old, in 52a he was 12 years old. Both examples are written in German. At the age of twelve he was highly sensitive. At this crucial period his self-respect experienced a hard blow (he was one of Hitler's victims), so that he suffers from a feeling of inadequacy with all its psychological implications. In trying to compensate for this negative self-feeling Charles sometimes appears assertive and self-satisfied in spite of his pronounced inner uncertainty. Being bumptious does not create a courageous attitude to life, and by being assertive Charles uses up too much of his energy, which should be directed to more useful channels.

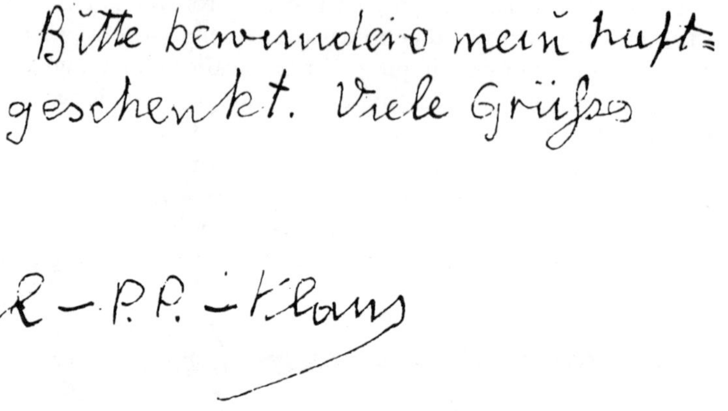

FIG. 52a

Too much energy is consumed by the young man's excessive use of self-control to conceal emotions the consequences of which he fears. Thus we see assertiveness and bumptiousness alternating with secretiveness and reticence, resulting in a loss of initiative and the power to stand up to opposition (see Fig. 52b). Charles is always spick and span, overconscientious and painstaking, always trying to make good, as if under a compulsion in spite of innate laziness. He goes all the way to appear as a hail-fellow-well-met, more for the sake of self assurance than to satisfy his vanity or ostentation.

On the one hand Charles appears to be placid, humble, resigned and almost apathetic; on the other he is restless under his outward tranquillity. Whenever his temper breaks out, it does so with a vengeance.

Though by no means of low intelligence, Charles has only a few potential interests. In some respect he is clever, but some of his efforts have a way of suddenly turning to inertia. Under these circumstances his prospects for a steady career are not promising.

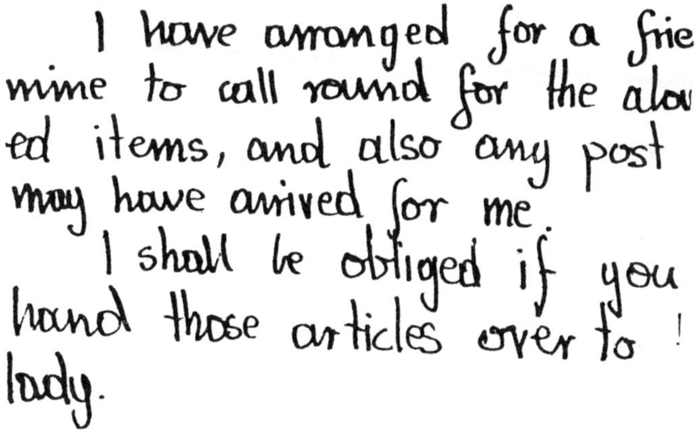

I have arranged for a frie
mine to call round for the alo
ed items, and also any post
may have arrived for me.
I shall be obliged if you
hand those articles over to !
lady.

FIG. 52b

Charles is not always straight and truthful. This deviousness and deceit are escape mechanisms due to fear. In spite of his many failings the boy is lovable for he is warm-hearted and kind. He should not be forced to climb too steep a hill or he will be tempted to take irrational short cuts. His awareness of his inferiority is intensified by his failure to solve his problems, and he is irritated by being too sheltered, he is undoubtedly an indulged son. He reacts in a sharp manner with the obstinacy and inconsideration of the selfish. Charles, at one and the same time, suffers from too many limitations and enjoys too many liberties. He needs to be encouraged to organise his life along sound and healthy lines. He needs security, recognition, freedom and power.

Since he shows a good sense of space and form he should be able to become a good draughtsman and find an opening in engineering concerns.

All cases of vocational guidance have a number of common factors. This should not be surprising as they are mostly due to the same fundamental difficulties, brought about by puberty and adolescence. The perplexities of this age do not always manifest themselves in the same way, however, but affect the young in various forms according to their disposition and environment. Sensitivity, a lack of security, intense anxiety, neurotic parental relations with a rejection of interference can be observed in most cases.

These difficulties have to be coped with, and if relieved at an early stage of development they can generally be overcome fairly easily. The young people can then enjoy a fuller life even during this critical period.

CHAPTER SIX

Symbols as Signposts

The personal pronoun 'I' stands for the ego, and the way in which a person shapes this letter is often highly significant. English grammar, alone of all the grammars in the world, decrees that this letter shall be written as a capital. Our enemies might ascribe this rule to our self-assertion; our friends will say that it shows our due self-respect.

Sign-reading is obsolete today, so the pronoun 'I' should never be studied alone. It has no significance except in so far as it is part of a whole manuscript. But an 'I' can be a most useful signpost and if the other features of a handwriting confirm its significance we are likely to understand the core of the writer's personality. The following examples of this pronoun suggest information, but accompanying graphological signs would have to decide its truth.

FIG. 53

Figure 53. This is the 'I' of the person in love with herself. The letter is almost twice as high as the 't' in 'must'. which should normally be only a little shorter than the 'I'. The writer doubtlessly considers herself very important.

FIG. 54

Figure 54 by way of contrast shows the 'I' of the person who suffers from an inferiority complex. The upper projection of the

letter 'f' in 'feeling' is double the height of the 'I' which ought to be equal in size.

$$\mathcal{I}\ am$$

FIG. 55

Figure 55 shows the 'I' of the accommodating and unsophisticated writer who does not impose upon others.

FIG. 56

Figure 56 stands for the negation of the ego which is due to a feeling of guilt.

FIG. 57

Figure 57 on the contrary shows the 'I' of a woman who expects more than her due. She spreads her ego and her personality.

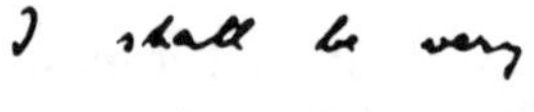

FIG. 58

Figure 58. shows the 'I' of the person who seeks solitude because she is a bad mixer.

FIG. 59

Figure 59 shows an 'I' written as a figure 9. This does not show an ability in mathematics, but it does suggest a love of money.

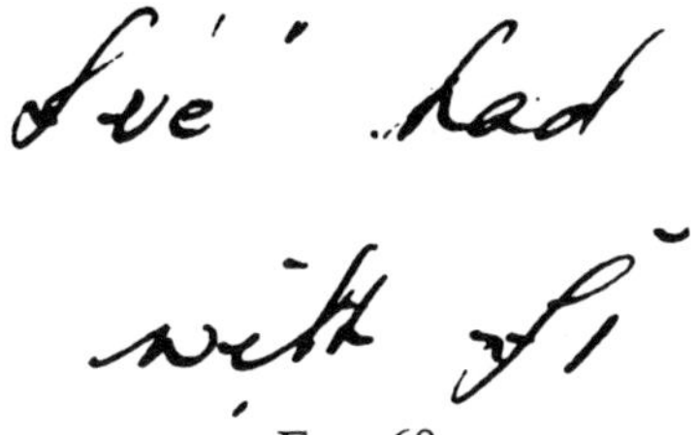

FIG. 60

Figure 60 also indicates an interest in money. The writer identifies herself with the £ sign which can be seen in the same sample.

FIG. 61

Figure 61 shows the 'I' of the cheerful person who greets you with an amiable wave of the hand. The author happens to know this young lady and she does in fact always greet her friends in the way indicated by her 'I'.

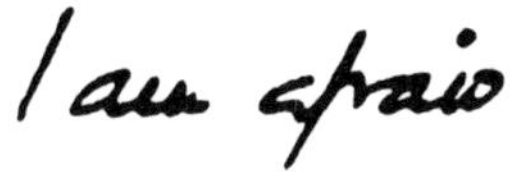

FIG. 62

Figure 62 shows an 'I' that is ostentatious in its simplicity. The writer is well aware of the fact that simple lines are becoming to her style of beauty.

FIG. 63

Figure 63 is an 'I' that gives evidence of the self-centred personality who moves around her own axis.

FIG. 64

Figure 64 is the insignificant 'I' of the individual endowed with an objective mind which is best suited for research work. The inclination towards narcissism which is shown in the meticulous exactitude of the formation of her 'I' is indicative of self-assertion in spite of apparent modesty.

FIG. 65

Figure 65 shows the piercing and aggressive 'I' of the self-righteous person who knows that attack is the most efficient form of self-defence.

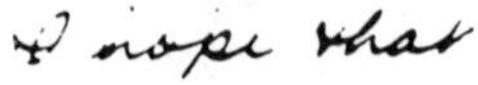

FIG. 66

Figure 66 is the typical 'I' of the American school-copy. It was produced by an American and has no significance with regard to the writer's character, but were we to find a similar formation in an English handwriting we should have to conclude that the writer leads the life of an oyster and refuses to come out of his shell.

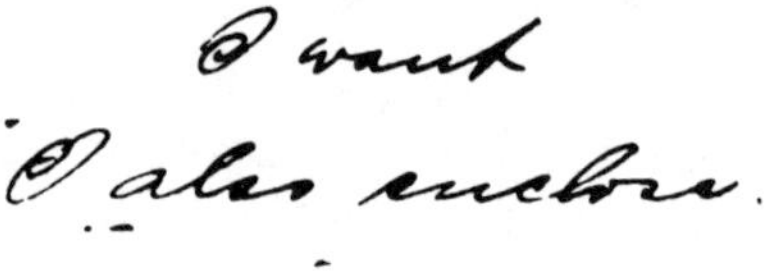

FIG. 67

Figure 67 shows the 'I' of a person who feels insecure and therefore seeks protection within himself against an unfriendly world.

FIG. 68

Figure 68 is a blatant example of a split personality. Note how the weak 'I' has been produced by several strokes of the pen and is at the same time shaky and frayed like the usual writing of people with frayed nerves. The disunity of this man's mind is discernible even to the uninitiated.

FIG. 69

Figure 69 shows an 'I' shaped like an ear. The writer is severely deaf and this organ-inferiority overshadows her personality.

Once more it must be emphasized that the analysis of a handwriting consists, as was shown in Chapter 2, of a close observation of the whole script. The 'I' must always be determined in this setting, but since it represents the ego no interpretation would be complete if special attention were not given to it. It often leads the handwriting-analyst in the right direction and is therefore of special significance.

Max Pulver, the eminent Swiss graphologist, once said, "Conscious writing is unconscious drawing." Conversely we might say that unconscious drawing, or 'doodling' reveals character as does conscious writing. Let us look at a few of these unconscious drawings.

FIG. 70

Figure 70 shows a drawing whose rigidity and asceticism are very significant. In a few lines of doodling this man has revealed his life-history. Brought up by a Puritan straight-laced mother, deprived of the warmth and affection essential for his emotional make-up particularly during his formative years, he fights his way through life's complexities. Discontented with himself, he resorts to a pointed resistance to the world at large, which is expressed in the sharply pointed elbow directed against his fellows. At the same time we note a certain sarcastic humour as of a man capable of laughing at himself. There is an alert and intelligent look which indicates the doodler's coherent mind, and the eyes of the drawing are like musical notes, betraying the man's interest in music.

FG. 71

These reflections, which were arrived at purely intuitively when the sketch was studied, were confirmed as correct by the doodler himself.

Figure 71 is also a doodle. The girl's thoughts are obviously chasing one another in incessant turmoil. Her interests are manifold, but none of them is compelling enough to lead her in the right direction. She is driven all over the place, not only because of difficulties and conflicts but also because of the unmatched temperaments of her parents which she has inherited and cannot integrate within herself. Intellectually she tries to repudiate her instinctive urges which she cannot completely ignore since there is a body-mind unity. Thus she creates more disharmony within herself, even to the significant extent of drawing her head apart from her body.

Figure 72 shows a doodle of fanciful formations to which only an intuitive interpretation can be given. To the author they suggest that the doodler has a constructive and brilliant mind, that he is artistic and musical and yet at the same time has a scientific bent. In spite of these outstanding gifts the man has a marked sense of reality, so that the practical and aesthetic aspects of his mind keep an even balance. He is wont to attend patiently to details, to be observant and to be keenly interested in his surroundings. He is an excellent draughtsman and sketches well. The geometrical symbols show a particular interest in architectural designs. The doodler is inclined to diffuse his energies because he has so many potentialities. It is evident that he is determined to hold the whip-hand in all situations in order to satisfy his ambitious nature. In this attempt he may even go too far at times in spite of his well-balanced judgment.

This man's ideas are versatile and are expressed in ever-changing patterns. He appears to be trying to free himself from himself and from the fetters of convention by giving rein to his unconscious mind. His designs fill the whole field of available space by sending out streamers of his thoughts and inventive imaginings. At the same time he displays a graceful elegance in a stylized and sophisticated mode of expression. The doodler is highly sexed and seems to have been crossed in love, an event of great importance in his mind.

FIG. 72

Many phallic symbols, as well as the pierced heart at the top of the drawing, lead to this bold statement.

This man is outstandingly gifted in figures, a fact which should stand him in good stead in his profession and at the same time prevent him from letting his fantasy run riot. Being blessed with so many potentialities and in addition with a high cultural standard, he has the opportunity of great success in whatever profession he may choose.

The recipient of this report, in acknowledging it, said, "You might be interested to learn that the gentleman in question is a Chartered Accountant. I have always considered him to be brilliant."

Markedly peculiar symbols are frequently to be seen in handwritings in which they make clear signposts which the graphologist follows up.

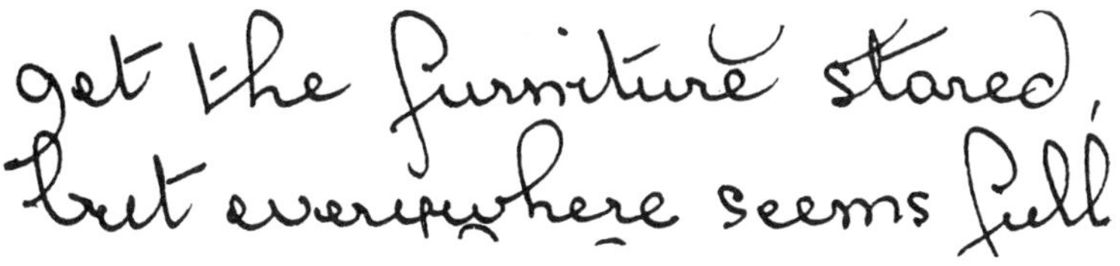

FIG. 73

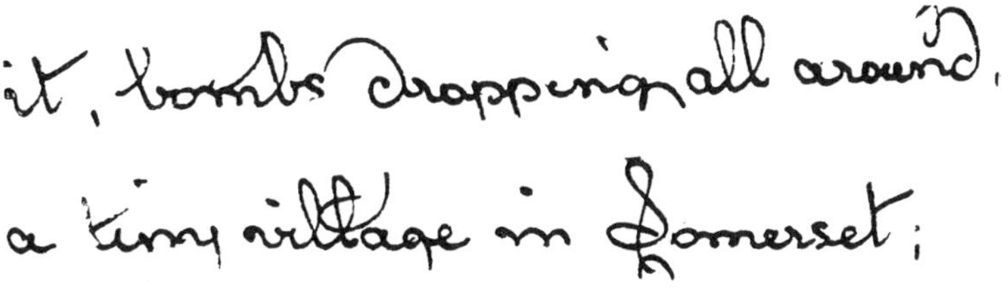

FIG. 74

Figures 73 and 74 show a handwriting which is interrupted with musical symbols. All the 'f's in Figure 73 e.g. 'furniture', 'full' are like the forte sign in music. In Figure 74 the 'd' in 'dropping' is formed like the symbol for a base clef while the capital 'S' in 'Somerset' is very like a reversed treble clef sign.

93

Figure 75 is supposed to read as '25 Pembridge'. The 2 in 25 is written in the shape of a heart. The writer likes to make a show

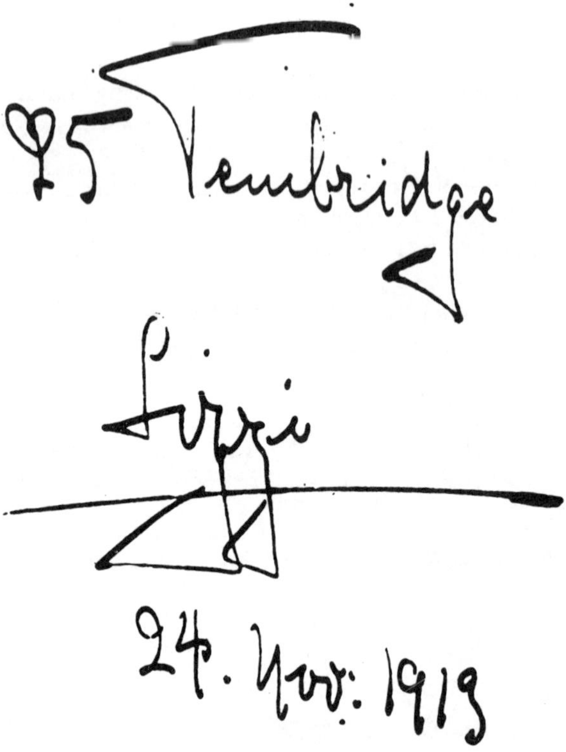

FIG. 75

of her emotions and would not shrink, in order to arouse the sympathy of the passer-by, from fixing a sign-post at her door indicating that this is the house of a woman with a pierced heart. This grotesque eccentricity is due to an exaggerated eroticism and excessive sentimentality. As a matter of fact, this woman committed suicide in a lunatic asylum. Her signature, very much to the left of the page, shows acute regression. The savage underlining crossing through the tails of the 'z's', is evidence of a desire to cancel herself out.

Figure 76 shows that even political views cannot be hidden from the graphologist. This is the writing of an Austrian cook who

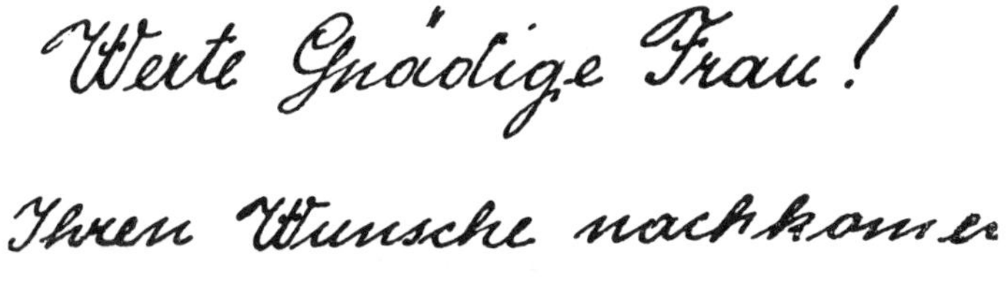

Werte Gnädige Frau!

Ihren Wunsche nachkommen

FIG. 76

applied for a situation in England before the second world war. The swastika can be seen in the 'W's and the 'F' in the specimen, and continues throughout the script. As the handwriting itself gave testimony of various undesirable qualities she did not get the position for which she applied.

and to post

FIG. 77

In Figure 77 a girl of thirteen in the throes of puberty, troubled with sadistic fantasies, draws unconsciously a man on a gallows in the words 'and to post.' Her aggression is directed against her father.

FIG. 78

Figure 78 shows an enlarged 'B' appearing in the signature of an expectant mother. The lady was perturbed at the change in her

95

signature and was at a loss to understand why it should suddenly take such dimensions. Undoubtedly she was very conscious of the change in her figure.

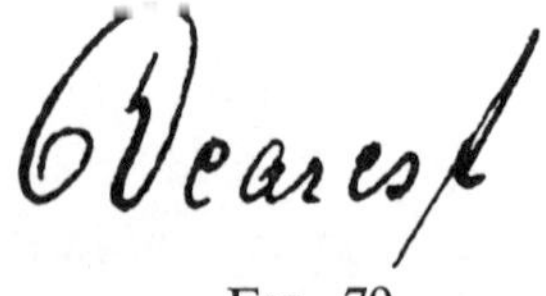

FIG. 79

Figure 79 shows the word 'Dearest' addressed by a lady to her friend when sending him greetings for his sixty-second birthday. The 62 in the capital 'D' is amazingly clear.

This interpretation of signs and symbols does not strictly speaking come under the heading of graphology. No short cuts in analyzing handwritings are reliable. However if we were to ignore symbols in handwritings we should lose useful signposts which may lead to conclusive interpretations.

Symbols by themselves, although never decisive, have an important bearing on the writer's personality. We have to go beyond the symbols to understand the unconscious processes of the mind. Should the assumptions arrived at by means of symbols remain unconfirmed when we group the graphological elements, the verdict they alone suggest would have to be modified.

CHAPTER SEVEN

Inebriety in Handwriting

There are 350,000 alcoholics in Britain and it is an established fact that excessive drinking can be found in all classes of society. These dipsomaniacs cause endless misery to others and moral disintegration as well as physical illness to themselves. Many of them become so ill mentally that they have to go into mental homes as alcoholic patients.

Knowing of the pernicious effects of excessive drinking the author undertook some research in the handwritings of alcoholics with the aim of finding the motives for giving way to excessive drinking and the degrees of inebriety as shown in handwritings. The finding of common features in those who derive pleasure from intoxication suggests the general conditions suitable for cure while the discovery of specific characteristics leads to individual diagnoses which have to be followed up by an attempted cure.

Alcoholism is not a vice but an illness. The alcoholic is not a moral weakling but a tragically sick person who, if his illness is recognized in its early stages, can be cured. Many inebriates have deep-seated psychological conflicts and if these conflicts can be brought to the patient's conscious mind and their origin explained, the afflicted person may be helped to recover. Until a cure is effected unhappiness leads to drinking, drinking to unhappiness, and the alcoholic and all those in his immediate circle are caught up in repeated misery.

Graphology can play a part in the search for the patient's maladjustment, and psychotherapy can frequently help the sufferer to normal conditions. There are many causes of inebriety. Heredity, environment, education, neglect, frustration or nervous causes such as anxiety or trauma may be responsible for the disorder. For example, spoilt children, who are unused to any opposition to their desires may turn into inebriates. On the other hand a too severe upbringing may lead to alcoholic indulgence as an escape from rigid discipline. Every case has to be investigated on its own merits. No generalisation accounts for all cases of drinking habits and no

97

single method of treatment will help all inebriates. A great deal depends on the personality of the inebriate and on his desire to be cured.

The task of the author was to find in the handwritings of alcoholic addicts common traits which might assist in differentiating the various degrees of alcoholism. The handwritings of the inmates of a Drink and Drug Addicts' Home were examined. After the patients' writings had been analyzed the matron of the home sent the case-histories so that it could be seen whether they corroborated the graphological findings. Some of the cases are now given here.

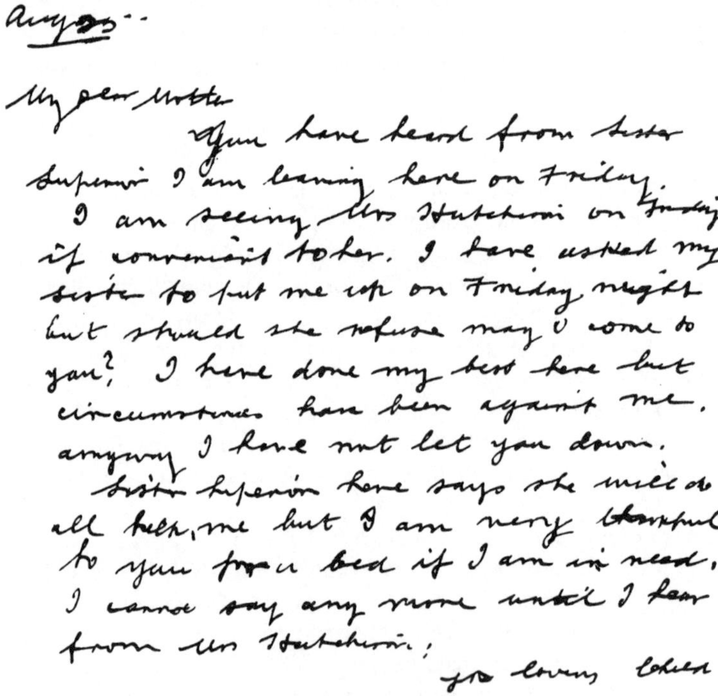

FIG. 80 (reduced)

The writing of the first patient, Mary, aged 35 years, which can be seen in Figure 80, gives a vivid picture of a disintegrated personality. It is jerky and shows frayed and mangled letter-formations.

The date, 'Aug. 25th' is smeary as well as shaky. The word 'Dear' addressing the recipient is small and unconvincing and the ending 'Your loving child' does not ring true. The correction in the first word of the letter, 'You', is superfluous and gives evidence of the writer's indecision. This is one of the symptoms frequently found in psychopathic cases. In spite of wavy lines, which denote instability, the writer never loses sight of her goal, but in the dark points in her initials, which show 'marking time' on paper, we recognize a feeling of guilt, and many of her 'I's', which stand for her ego, are remarkably small showing doubt of her own value. There is a peculiar formation in her 'I' in line 6 of the text: the 'I' of 'May I come?' was written with several strokes of the pen and mirrors a most pitiful personality.

The writing shows general intelligence apart from the frequent distortions affecting the legibility which prove that the writer is afraid to express herself clearly. A defective muscular control is partly responsible for this shortcoming and many sudden interruptions show the writer's irregular rhythm. The dark colour and general heaviness of this cheerless and sinister script express a morbid mentality.

In spite of all the depressed and depressing symptoms there are indications that Mary is eager to mend her ways. Note, for example, the small corrected 'I' in line 11. This woman is continually in conflict with herself and so is unable to solve her problems. The result is irritability and capriciousness which in her writing is expressed in sharp and sudden angular formations such as the 'v' in 'Have' (lines 9 and 10). She uses all sorts of connections, a trait which in a low standard writing indicates weakness of character.

The character-sketch of the patient, Mary, suggested by her handwriting is that the woman is a cramped, sulky and dejected individual who cannot adapt herself to her surroundings and is very difficult to cope with. An unstable and unbalanced disposition dominates her actions. In spite of a feeling of guilt and frustration she is self-righteous, obstinate and exceptionally touchy, particularly when she suspects that she is being slighted.

The writer's craving for alcohol seems to be of long standing and has impaired her capacity for normal development. She is handi-capped physically as well as morally for she lacks co-ordinated movements, a condition that causes delayed reactions. Her will-power, which is demonstrative at times, remains ineffective in reality. She is in the throes of an overpowering constraint which precludes any objective judgment. All the same, she wants to improve as her frequent corrections show. By trying to be as inconspicuous as possible she hopes to avoid observation of her failure. She is an habitual drink-addict and no marked improve-ment can be expected.

Unpleasant childhood experiences seem to have fostered the craving for alcohol in this woman. When she gave way to the craving she began to feel inferior and so gradually lost faith and self-respect.[1]

The case-history of the patient Mary as given by the matron said:

"The patient is a manic depressive psychotic and a real dipso-maniac. She is a most tragic case, as in the upgrade she is a splendid character, honest, hardworking, capable and intelligent. She is definitely attractive to women and as far as we know never had any male friends, which we notice is often the case with dipsomaniacs. Since we have known her she has had a definite rhythm. During the spring and summer she is a trustworthy, happy and hardworking woman. In the autumn she gets depressed, sus-picious, discontented and bad-tempered. She then recalls splendid episodes of the past in which she figured as a genius and leader. (We have not found much ground for these memories.) She con-siders it a disgrace that anyone so capable should be doing so little with her life and she runs away secretly with no apparent sense of honour or dues to us. Sometimes in the winter she comes back again in varying degrees of shame and disaster and is overwhelmed with despair.'"

The next writing, Figure 81, is that of the patient Winnie, aged 65 years. It shows the contradictory nature of a person who moves

---

1 The letter which was analyzed was evidently written in Mary's down-grade, for the positive qualities mentioned in the matron's report cannot be observed in this particular script. Author.

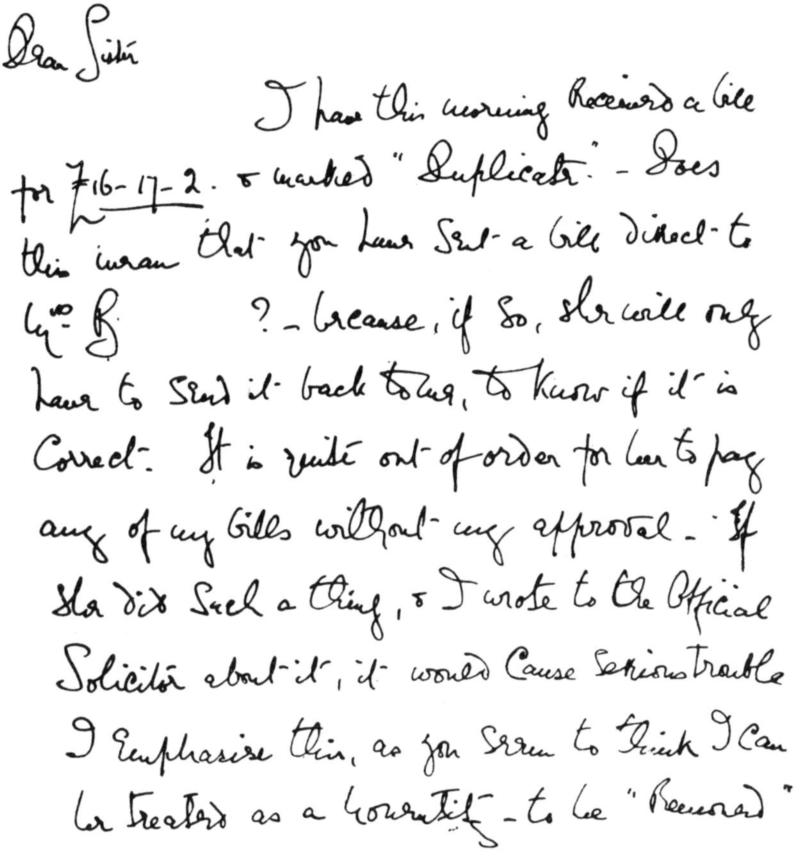
Dear Sister
I have this morning Received a bill
for £16-17-2. & marked "Duplicate" - Does
this mean that you have Sent a bill direct to
Mrs B ? - because, if so, she will only
have to Send it back to me, to know if it is
Correct. It is quite out of order for her to pay
any of my bills without my approval. - If
she did such a thing, & I wrote to the Official
Solicitor about it, it would Cause serious trouble
I Emphasise this, as you seem to think I can
be treated as a nonentity - to be "Removed"

FIG. 81 (reduced)

in extremes. The formation of her 'I' is enlarged but it is crossed through in the upper part of the letter. Observe the first 'I' of the script and the 'I' in line 8 of the text which express a disregard for herself and her life in spite of her pompous display and affected manner. If we compare the 'S' in 'Sister' with the 's' in the insignificant word 'is' (line 6), we get the essence of her character. Whatever she does is showy and ostentatious and has to be in full view, but matters that she considers unimportant are completely neglected, because the patient lacks a sense of proportion. The sinking lines prove that her verve is merely 'window-dressing'. The small 'e's' are written in the Greek form to give herself a façade of culture and sophistication, while her capital 'D's', as in 'Duplicate' and 'Dues' (line 2) show an extraordinary selfishness and a narcissistic tendency. Good manual dexterity and great skill are needed for these complicated formations. The writer is by no means a humdrum personality, but is inventive and original. It is all the more deplorable to find her potentialities impoverished by alcohol.

There are many more contradictions in this script. Note, for example, the word 'such' (line 8) and compare it with the words 'to me' and 'to know' (line 5) with their overconnections, a difference denoting irrationality and irritability. The word 'nonetity' (line 11), when the meaning of the word is taken into consideration, is particularly striking in its distortion, for the angle is quite irregular and the final letter 'y' looks pitiful in its twisted formation. All Winnie's pretended vitality and power have vanished at this point, leaving only a shaky scrawl which cannot be read but has to be surmised. An additional symptom of her condition is the small upper margin, whereby the patient expresses her disrespect for the recipient of the letter.

The character sketch of the patient, Winnie, suggested by her handwriting is that of a woman who is pathologically vain. She is smart, clever and versatile but all her abilities only serve her exaggerated ambitions. She is bound to disappoint anyone who takes her at her face value. Her self-evaluation is pitched too high, with the result that a sober estimate or, worse still, a hostile criticism of her would affect her severely. She cannot reach the goal she has set herself, partly owing to advanced age and partly to moral weakness, so she plays out her desire in vivid fantasies. Her imagination carries her away into her world of make-believe, an exalted world where she is her own spectacle and her own spectator. Her paranoid self-centredness obscures her judgment for a time, but when she comes down to earth her troubled mind drives her to despair and she even feels inclined at times to strike herself out of existence. The script sent for examination was written in a state of acute excitement and annoyance, a mood which made her boisterous, quarrelsome, aggressive and turbulent.

The cause of this woman's alcoholism appears to lie in an over-protected, pampered and spoilt childhood. Selfish and distressed by the rebuffs of life, she took to drink to soothe her injured ego. She is the self-indulgent alcohol fiend, the pleasure-seeker who gives way to her inclinations without any sort of moral resistance.

The case-history of the patient Winnie as given by the matron said:

"This patient did well except for violent outbursts of temper. She left us to take a post but returned six months later, having been drinking again, very unbalanced and nervous. She made no attempts to settle, but was defiant, secretive and untruthful, and in the end left suddenly to go back to her home. Later she was found unconscious, having tried to gas herself. She was then taken to a mental hospital. Her history since her discharge has been one of periods of being quite normal except for outbursts of temper. She has been a capable and clean worker, but one who has relapses into instability, moodiness and depression, followed by another fit of alcoholism."

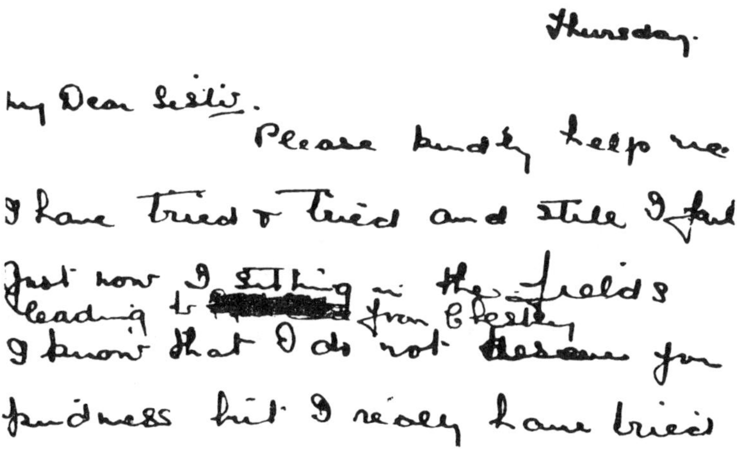

FIG. 82 (reduced)

Figure 82 shows the writing of the patient, Jane, who was 33 years old. A jerky unrest is expressed in this script in the shaky letters, an exaggerated tendency to the left, many corrections and an uncertain stroke-impulse resulting in letters written with varied types of stroke. The i-dots are all over the place, a symptom of lack of concentration, and there are broken strokes and in places a tapering off of the pressure as well as an inconsistent slant and an irrational style. Omissions, errors and retracings give evidence of a troubled mind, and the exceedingly small 'I's' (line 2 and line 5) which are formed like embryos are symbolic of a development arrested at an early stage. The whole picture of this script suggests an unbalanced temperament and a neurotic disposition.

The character-sketch of the patient, Jane, suggested by her handwriting is that of a blatant case of physical and moral disintegration. The patient comes from a poor background and evidently had a very hard childhood. Frustration and deprivation are responsible for her lust to steal from life her fair share of the good things that have been denied her. She is untruthful in word and action and quite unreliable. Her aggressive manner is the result of her frustration. She seems to be entangled in her difficulties and is dimmed, muddled and distracted, so that she is quite incapable of logical thought. Altogether life seems to have very little happiness in store for her and therefore it bewilders and frightens her.

The patient is severely discontented with life. She has suffered from deprivations and an unstable background from her earliest childhood and all her efforts to get more from life have come to naught. Jane was life's step-child, so she had to find some form of compensation. The only cheerfulness she has ever experienced has been brought about by alcohol. The reaction to this artificial happiness, however, is deep depression, a disturbed mind and a loss of self-respect. Thus she goes from bad to worse.

The case-history of Jane as given by the matron said:

"This patient was born in Australia. Her father was a mining engineer and the family had a most unsettled life roaming about, the children getting a sketchy education wherever they happened to be. The family tradition was not one of strict morality and from the age of seventeen Jane had 'adventures'. She is twice divorced and has one illegitimate child. She has gradually become more and

104

more addicted to alcohol, which was probably taken at first to keep herself going.

Jane was a most difficult patient while with us, finding it impossible to keep the rules. She was bad-tempered, suspicious and quarrelsome. She could not settle to any definite work and the financial question was urgent. She left to take a place as a housekeeper where she could have her child with her. We have not heard from her for a considerable time and we are not very hopeful of a successful career having been established."

Figures 83 and 84 show the handwritings of two patients, Daisy aged 43 and Ruth aged 54, who were closely linked together. They are of interest from the point of view of their friendship and therefore have to be considered in terms of their mutual relationship.

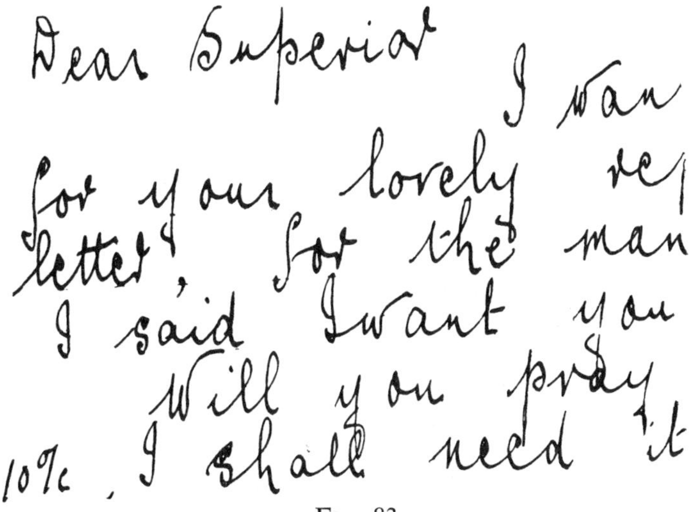

FIG. 83

Daisy's writing shows a constrained, rigid, painstaking and elaborate caligraphy. The bizarre formations are typical of an hysteric. Her character can be clearly seen as marked by pathological insincerity and a mixture of subtle intrigue and naive immaturity. The perverted mannerism and the lability are prominent. Sharp and sudden angles in the writing suggest aggression, lack of consideration for others and obstinacy, qualities which are not likely to go well with her friend's changeable moods. Daisy tries to impress, using all the means at her disposal, but the irregularity in the size of her letters and in the pressure, and the wavy lines give proof of her instability. In order to ingratiate herself with others and satisfy her own vanity and desire for self-assertion, she tries to keep up an artificial standard but cannot manage it for long. When she feels utterly 'on the rocks' she likes to make a scene and behave in a spectacular manner. Daisy is not of a high educational standard; in fact she has not increased her knowledge since her schooldays. Owing to her lack of moral resistance she resorts again and again to alcohol, hoping that it may give her strength to brave life adequately, not realizing that she is defeating her own ends thereby.

In the patient Daisy, we see the meticulous person, sensitive, frightened, insecure and cautious, As an anodyne to harsh reality she needs a stimulant to increase her courage for life. She is a lonely introvert, and because she feels stronger under the influence of alcohol she believes that her salvation lies in its consumption.

The case-history of Daisy as given by the matron said:

"The patient has been in and out of this home since 1937, and had been in various inebriate homes before that trying to pull up. She suffered from cardiac asthma on any exertion and it is not unlikely that these pains caused her to become addicted to alcohol. She has always been a difficult patient, very discontented, always feeling neglected and wrongly treated, and being a great mischief-maker among the nurses. She is a plain little woman, but has been a smart dress-maker and knows how to make the best of herself. She is full of self-pity and no care or attention is received gratefully. Last time she was here she went away with one of her bosom friends (Ruth), who had become absolutely infatuated with her. She has recently been drinking heavily again, Eau de Cologne if she has nothing else."

The most noteworthy feature in the writing of the other patient, Ruth, is her 'I's'. The first letters in Figure 84, lines 7 and 8, portray a pitiful, utterly dejected person. Some of her 'I's' are written in the form of question marks as if the writer were questioning herself, asking why she lives and what point there is in her life. Weak nerves and a poor physique are additional causes for her feeling of inadequacy. She manages to express herself with the least possible effort. Her letters are over-simplified and incomplete and yet legible. The irregularity in size, pressure and letter-formation are indicative of her irritable and unbalanced disposition. Her

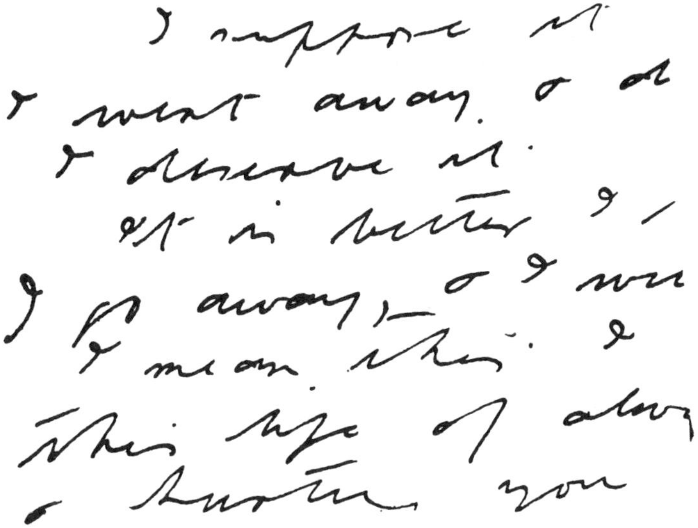

FIG. 84

reasoning power does not seem to be impaired by alcohol, for she has an unusual gift for combining letters and writing logically. The word 'shortcomings' (figure 84a), for example, is produced without interruption, and is most skilfully connected. Only a cunning person can construct so artful a combination.

FIG. 84a

The character-sketch of the patient Ruth as suggested by her writing is that of a woman of pronounced intelligence. Her resourceful 'couldn't care less' attitude stands in complete contrast to

Daisy's cramped tension. Ruth is certainly not a strong personality, but there is something peculiarly masculine about her. She seems to be a conundrum to herself and to those around her. Utterly defenceless, she surrenders to every impulse without compunction. She is morbidly afraid of life, and fear produces an inner urge to escape from danger which drives her from pillar to post. She seems to have no roots and to be completely detached from her past. This leads to the inference that she has never been blessed with a sheltered home and therefore drifts without plan or purpose. Ruth's writing suggests that she was of more than average intelligence before she became a prey to alcohol, and is even now exceptionally logical in her lucid moments. Her rhythm, however, is disturbed. At times she walks about like a shadow so that she can hardly be noticed. Her mind dwells on all sorts of plans as to how best she may escape from reality, but as she rarely carries out any of her projects it is to be hoped that she will fail to fulfil her self-destructive intentions.

The patient Ruth is morally and physically disintegrated to such an extent that she is barely conscious of her actions. She is in a state of exhaustion and is only a shadow of her former self, leading a life so futile as to be hardly worth living. She gives way to all her impulses and falls easily under the sway of undesirable influences. Her first error was to succumb to alcohol which poisoned her system; now she cannot resist it.

Daisy, who is of a perverted and receptive sensuality, seems to be as much under the spell of Ruth as Ruth is attracted by her. Daisy approves, in Ruth, of all the qualities which are lacking in her own make-up. Ruth is definitely masculine so much so that it is difficult to persuade ourselves that a woman has written her letter.

Evidently it is this contrast which constitutes the bond between the two women and their reciprocal attraction. In practice it is unlikely that these two friends can support one another since their friendship is built only on their instinctive tendencies. Both lack moral strength and the control of their impulses. The outcome can only be a surrender to their weaknesses. Ruth has not enough courage to face life squarely nor enough force of character to carry her plans to a successful end. She is dominated by an overwhelming sense of futility and insecurity and is therefore lamentably helpless in practical issues. This friendship is bound to be shipwrecked: a separation would be merciful.

The case of Ruth as given by the matron said:

"This patient was brought to us by her sister, who had returned from South Africa to find her leading a most irregular life, drinking, frequenting night-clubs and indulging in every form of immorality. Ruth appears to be an intellectual and almost masculine character. She was appreciative of help and could interest herself in good literature. She has a real appreciation of spiritual things and found that religion supplied a great lack in her life.

Unfortunately she became passionately attached to Daisy and soon deteriorated visibly. It was almost impossible to believe that a middle-aged woman could be so silly. She lost all regard for appearances, all interest in other things, and became the abject slave of this other woman, breaking rules and disregarding all considerations of honour to please her. Ruth apparently has had similar friendships before.

She is of the typist class, but married a continental count who soon became tired of her and is himself an immoral character. She was divorced by her husband and went back to her parents. The patient left us immediately her friend did and tried to live with her 'to help her keep straight,' which of course ended in both of them drinking together. In the end there was an abrupt termination of their friendship with much disillusion. The patient was however never bitter, though terribly disappointed in her friend. She is now back with us again, but is already showing signs of making fresh attachments. She is of a slothful, sensual temperament and, although inclined to shrink from any free social mingling, she likes to be one of a small coterie who spend all their free time playing cards and smoking, when not kept at some form of work or active exercise. She is honestly trying to recover and in spite of a sharp temper and openly shown annoyance when not allowed her own way does not bear malice after an incident. Unfortunately she has quite a habit of gravitating to the most undesirable of our patients whose company I suppose requires none of that effort she is too lazy to make."

The handwriting of the next patient, Molly aged 66, can be seen in Figure 85. It is the product of a complicated character. In spite of a few shaky strokes it shows comparative firmness and suggests a much younger person. The letter formation is pleasant but not easily legible. The distance between words is fairly wide and suggests a predilection for solitude. The page is, however crowded and

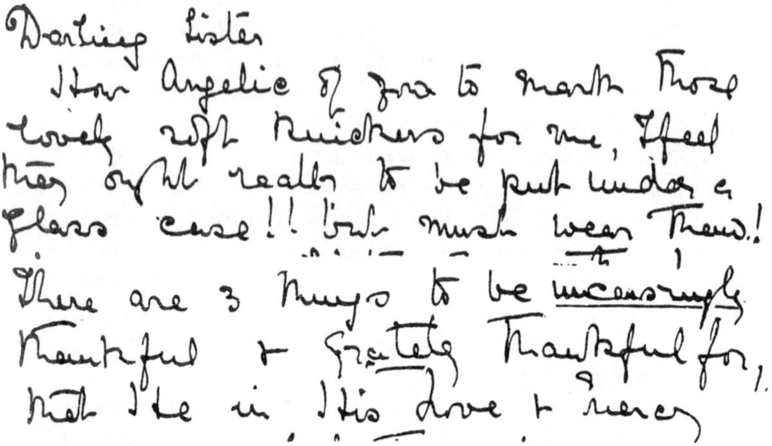

FIG. 85

lacks the normal conventional margins. The style is artificial, pretending to be that of a lady of culture of a high standard. The script, in its careful yet constrained execution, suggests that we are dealing with a person of high principles, good education and aesthetic feeling. The writer's sensitiveness is expressed in weak pressure while the varied forms of connections speak of versatility. A pronounced tendency to the left is usually found in selfish people. Frequent overconnections intermingled with unnecessary interruptions show an unbalanced temperament. The duplication of the exclamation mark after the word 'case' and the underlining of 'unceasingly' as well as 'greatly' are the reactions of an exalted personality. The initials are overemphasized and ornamented in contrast with the neglected middle letters; externalities obviously play an important part in her mind.

The character-sketch of the patient Molly as suggested by her writing is that of a woman with many contraditions and conflicts within herself. She is depressed and elated, sincere and sancti-monious—in fact a whole battery of contradictory adjectives could be used in describing her unusual make-up. In many ways she is daring and blunt in approach, yet she has difficulties in coping with ordinary situations.

Molly is quite convinced of her abilities and sure of herself, yet she is weighed down by a severe feeling of guilt which depresses her to such an extent that she contemplates suicide. Her optimism however comes to the rescue; besides she feels compelled to keep up the family prestige, though having come down in the world she does not always succeed and her conceit is often the only thing left of her tradition. In spite of her failings she manages to create a good impression and in her pleasant moods she is most likeable. She expected solace and a solution of her difficulties from indul-gence in alcohol. Having given way to this evil practice she can now no longer resist temptation.

Molly, an over-conscientious and highly-principled woman, whose ego-ideal cannot endure the weakness of her real character, lacks the magnanimity of soul to forgive herself. Driven to despair she took to drink to drown her sorrow. Her initial liking for alcohol was fostered by the relief from anxieties that it gave her. After years of indulgence in alcohol she has become an obsessional person moving in a stereotyped manner.

The case history of the patient Molly as given by the matron said:

"Molly, aged 66 years, with the figure and complexion, after hours of make-up, of a girl of 23, has been in and out of this home for the last twenty years or more. She has been an actress (not very successful) and is very musical. She also had one or two attempts at training for a nurse and did two years at one of the well-known hospitals. She is of good Scottish stock. In spite of many sordid episodes and a varied life, she has never lost her joie de vivre and a real childlike trust of soul. She is immaculate as to chastity, never having had any interest in sex. She is a splendid nurse —or was; she is now getting too blind to see the thermometer and too deaf to hear calls. But her self-conceit is amazing; she thinks she is quite sublime at everything she does. She openly gives out that her only failing in any respect is this tiresome addiction to the 'little glass of port', which is always attributed to the devil. If she is ever detected drinking, she leaves at once as her pride cannot stand the faintest criticism, but after weeks or even months of being missing, she turns up again somehow from somewhere, and we start all over again. Everyone loves Molly, and the fiction of her splendid career is pandered to by all in face of any evidence to the contrary. Everything is melodramatic with Molly, even if she is talking of suicide. One cannot take her seriously, yet she is tragic as she is so lovable and has made such a hash of her life."

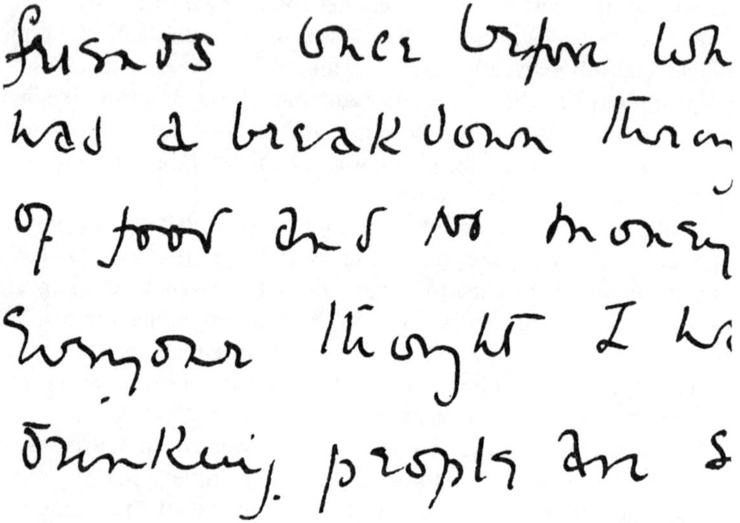

FIG. 86

Figure 86 shows the handwriting of the patient Sonia, aged 40. At first sight it makes a good impression and one feels inclined to judge favourably the writer who is without doubt an unusually interesting and outstanding personality. We can see her upbringing and her pleasant yet rather nonchalant manner. She is highly intelligent, has manifold interests, good artistic and literary appreciation and is gifted in poetry, music and all the visual arts. Considering her versatile abilities she ought to do great things, but lack of perseverance and diligence curb her potentialities. Being a born improvisator she makes life as easy as possible for herself. She is inconsiderate and selfish and expects to be the centre of attraction. She is an extraverted type and whenever she finds a congenial response she is amiable and pleasant; failing this response her moods can be unbearable. In spite of her attempts to curb her aggressive tendencies, there is always the chance that she may pick a quarrel at any moment. She is expansive in social situations and talks to anyone whoever she may be without making lasting contacts. At best she succeeds in making formal surface friendships. Convinced of her charm she brings her power into play. She is quite unscrupulous in narrative owing to her vivid imagination, but she is a keen calculator particularly in money matters and takes every opportunity to enrich herself for she is mercenary and extravagant. Her fantasies serve to bolster up her ego, for her irrational sense of proportion prompts her to expect too much of life. Her mind is accomplished and refined, but her character is weak. She is easily misled and reacts to bad influence without moral resistance, so that her reliability is always doubtful. She shows a superficial carelessness and a self-indulgence in pleasure-seeking. Having been pampered all her life she has difficulty in adapting herself to circumstances. She is used merely to express a wish in order to be obeyed.

Although erotic, Sonia repudiates a normal sexual outlet and male admiration merely serves her vanity. Her energies all seem to be concentrated on the one idea of how best she can get her own way. This condition sets up unnecessary tension. Her character, though attractive by its many sparkling facets, should be faced with caution.

Sonia's case history is not available, but the matron wrote in answer to this report, 'Patient Sonia is an interesting woman and a big problem. Your handwriting analysis is quite excellent.'

In the course of the study of inebriate handwritings it became possible to determine the causes which brought these unfortunate women to drink. From a careful examination of the graphological symptoms it can be concluded that biological, emotional and mental dispositions all lead to alcoholic indulgence. Somatic as well as functional disorders are quite clearly shown but it is difficult to say which is cause and which effect. The motives for taking to alcohol vary and only one point seems to be pertinent to all the cases. All these inebriates shrink from facing their difficulties and solving their problems. This may be the underlying cause of all inebriety, drinking in itself being only a symptom of a deeply-seated maladjustment.

The common features found in the handwritings of the inebriates were lack of self-control, self-indulgence, irritability, instability, unreliability, mendacity, obstinacy and self-centredness.[1] In some cases incoherent thinking, delusions and physical and mental disintegration could also be detected. As many of the patients were middle-aged the sex problem could generally be excluded although some perversions were in evidence.

No single situation can be held responsible for the addict's degeneration. Matrimonial difficulties, frustration at home or in work, straitened circumstances, sex misguidance, traumatic experiences in early childhood, the feeling of dejection, ineffectual efforts and many other causes can lead to inebriety. As is borne out by most of the case histories, life did not run smoothly for these unfortunates.

It should be noted that the common factors found in the foregoing handwritings are not relevant only to alcoholic indulgence, but to almost all psychopathic cases. No specific factor pertinent only to alcoholism has been found.

---

1 All the complexes will be found in the Appendix in alphabetical order, pp. 172-183.

CHAPTER EIGHT

Mental Disturbances Expressed in Handwriting

Psychopathic cases show in their handwritings many of the symptoms already noted in cases of inebriety but also some that are different. A few examples are given in this chapter.

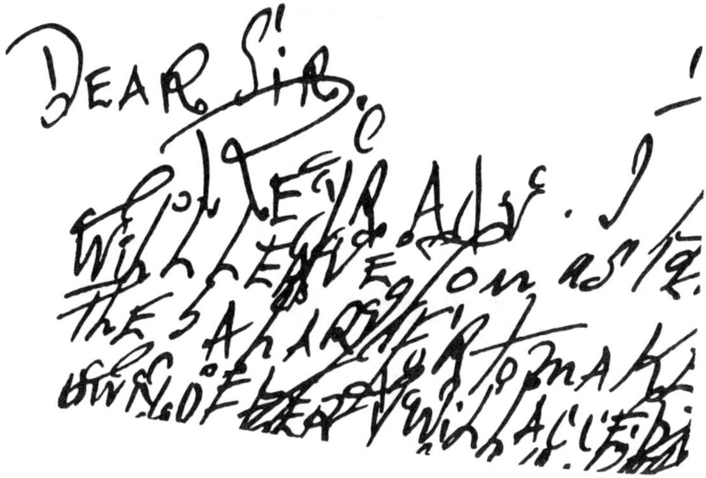

FIG. 87

Only a glance at Figure 87 is enough to give the observer a feeling of giddiness. This writing, almost staggering to the healthy-minded, shows that the writer's mind is in a whirl. His thoughts are thrown onto the paper in such rapid succession that one thinks of a kaleidoscope without its colour or symmetry. There are hardly any rounded forms to be seen, but sharp angular letters abound, giving evidence of violent aggression in a hopeless scatterbrain.

This writing presents the sinister picture of a severely afflicted schizophrenic whose provocative outbursts are not without their danger. It is almost inconceivable that a man in such a very bad state of confusion should not be under supervision. His letter is the answer to an advertisement for a private secretary. He offers his

115

services for the position and wishes his prospective wife to be established as a cashier at the same time. He suggests a joint salary and says that he is a good typist and shorthand-writer. It is, however, hardly possible to decipher what he has to say, and it is doubtful if he will be offered the position.

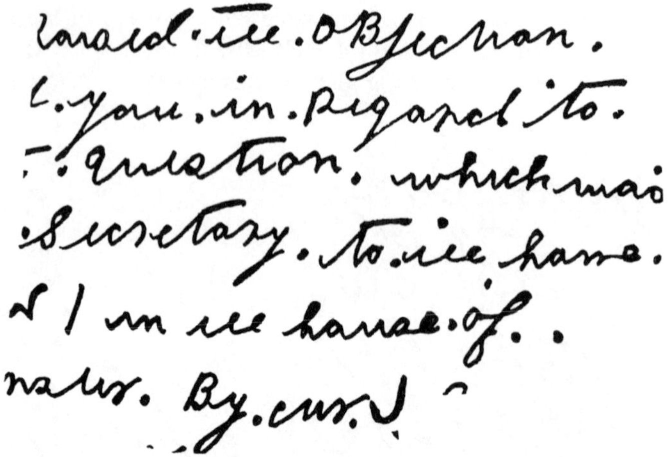

FIG. 88

Figure 88 is another blatant example of a psychotic handwriting which must be diagnosed as a case of dementia praecox. The stereotyped and arrested movements and the disturbed rhythm pertinent to this particular form of mental disease can easily be observed. Words and strokes are duplicated, a form of writing analogous to the psychotic's repetitive words and movements.

The frequent full stops, graphologically termed resting-points, indicate lapses and an interrupted flow of the writer's mode of expression. These resting-points are very significant. The writer gapes and feels lost while the pen rests on the paper producing dots and giving at the same time evidence of the discontinuity of his trend of thought. The immaturity of the script is an additional symptom of his regression.

Figure 89 is the handwriting of a man who suffers from a delusion of grandeur or megalomania. A sense of proportion is completely lacking and the regression into childhood is striking and

116

alarming. This man, originally a highly cultured person who holds the distinction of a B.Sc., has been in an asylum for nearly fifteen years and his chance of recovery is small.

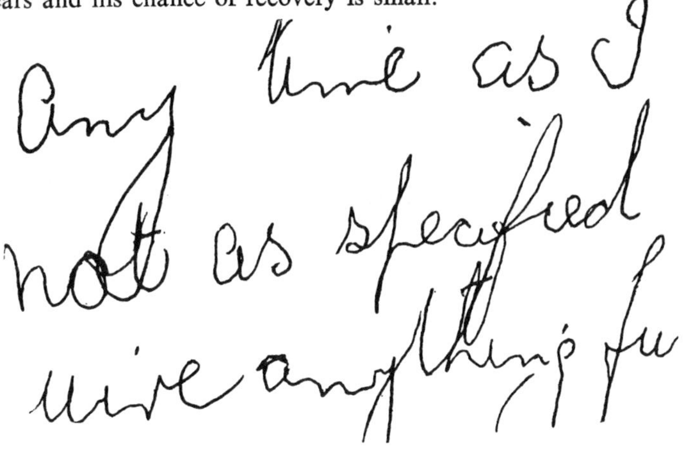

FIG. 89

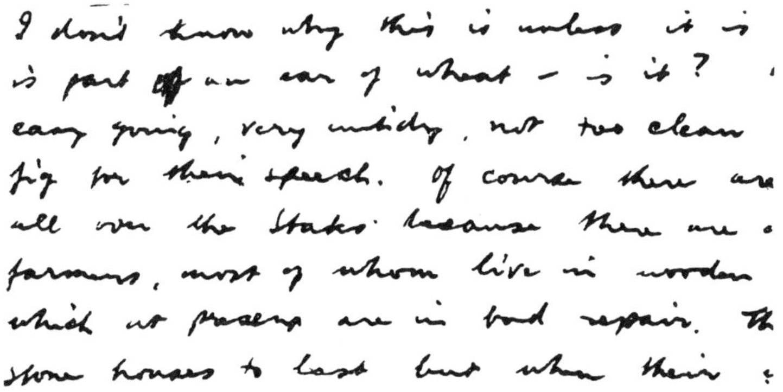

FIG. 90

Figure 90[1] shows the writing of a man of 38. It is an extremely small hand, shaky and broken, with mangled strokes and, generally speaking, no pressure. Such a writing indicates a sensitivity that is not healthy. The script is still legible but shows all the symptoms of mental and physical disintegration.

1 Only part of this manuscript is reproduced here.

The writer of this script is a paranoic, that is to say he suffers from a persecution mania. It is surprising that a man so afflicted is still capable of keeping a straight line in his handwriting. The fact that he does so is a sign that in spite of his illness there is a tenacity of purpose left. Similarly, though his mode of expression is dim and blurred the spacing of his letter is not impaired but shows that his conventional upbringing is still standing him in good stead. The underlining of words and some superfluous exclamation marks give evidence of an exalted state of mind, while the corrections, a common symptom of psychotic cases, are numerous. Sudden and irregular pressure, inconsistent interruptions and disconnections, as well as some peculiar letter-formations lead to the same conclusion.

A report based on this script was made about the writer. It said, 'Mr. C. is a highly cultured man with refined and aesthetic tastes and literary abilities. His potentialities, however, have not been developed to the full because of his state of health. He is not capable of an original effort and is not sufficiently stung by any failure to try again. He occupies himself only with congenial affairs and anything requiring discipline is brushed aside as objectionable.

The writer's mind is far too inconsistent and too romantic to be termed healthy, and his delicately-knit structure with its degenerated refinement must come to grief sooner or later. To ensure strictly limited responsibilities the man seeks a life of seclusion and keeps up the role of an indulged child. Avoiding social contacts and the bustle of life, he hankers after self-delusive fantasies.

Mr. C. is an unassuming, shy, retiring person, but he will always insist on his point of view. Under this cloak of persistence he is trying to hide his effeminate disposition. He imagines that between him and the world there exists a painful antagonism endangering his ego. The effects of this antagonism are apparent in a feeling of anxiety, sudden anger or even hate. Inner conflict inhibits the writer's instinctive urges. He has a high ego-ideal but a negative judgment of his personality. The difference between the claims of his conscience and his actual achievements gives him a feeling of guilt and tension. Logical thought does not help him for he cannot keep it up and it alternates with distorted images.

This case has gone too far for the employment of a psychotherapist, but a psychiatrist should be consulted. Disintegration has set in at a very early age in the mental and in the somatic sphere.

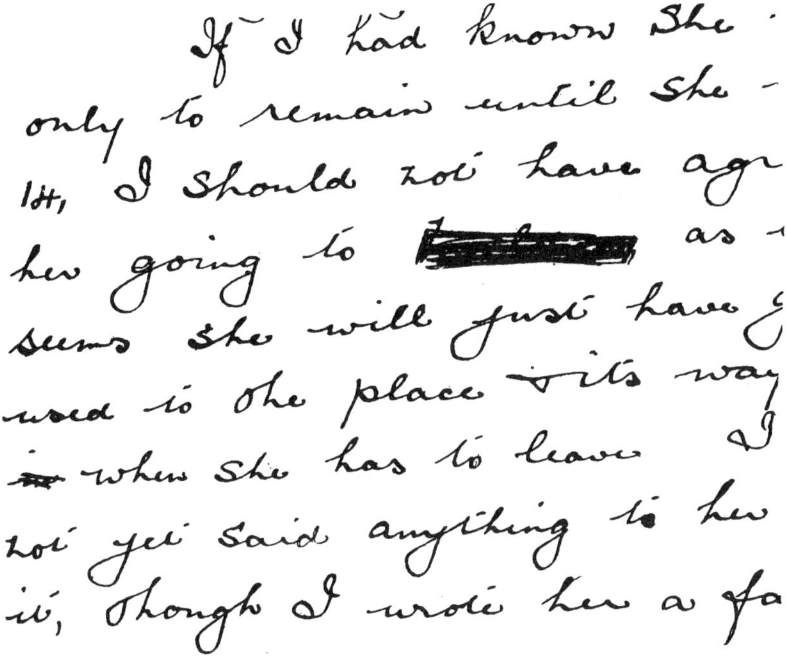

FIG. 91

Figure 91 shows the writing of Mrs. W. The Department of Education of a city in the Midlands required information about her character because she was the mother of two of their charges whose future had to be decided. Could these children be entrusted to their mother or would it be better for them to be cared for in an institution? This case is of particular interest because the graphological report is corroborated by the complete case history.

An analysis, similar to that carried out in Chapter 2, was made of Mrs. W.'s writing and revealed a character structure which was reported in these words:

Mrs. W. is a highly neurotic person, who, although infantile and immature in many ways, is very subtle in gaining her own ends.

She can ingratiate herself with a benevolent gesture, is talkative and entertaining for the sake of becoming a favourite and has winning ways and a playful lability. At times, however, she is blunt, inconsiderate and obstinate, and she rarely acts spontaneously but views a situation with a cold and diplomatic artfulness, her plans and projects being well-premeditated. Expecting more than her due, Mrs. W. often seizes her opportunity to make presumptuous and expansive demands on those surrounding her and is disappointed if she cannot get all she counted on. In periods of stress she makes exaggerated parasitic claims on society, at the same time shrinking from the effort of accepting her own share of responsibility. She has two different measures of judgment, one for herself and another for her friends. She is of a morbid state of mind, has a vague fear of life and is rather queer in some of her reactions. By means of nonchalant or naive behaviour she camouflages her inner uncertainty, giving herself the appearance of verve and vitality though she has none. She is fundamentally lethargic with a definite leaning to inertia. She is frequently involved in controversy, deriving a certain amount of satisfaction from playing one party off against the other. This is one of the main reasons for her difficulty in making social contacts. Convinced of her superiority and foolishly devoid of self-criticism, she is inclined to look down on others. In her elated states she makes sweeping statements because she lacks logic and jumps to far-fetched conclusions.

Mrs. W. is not as generous as she pretends to be; she tries to appear as a giver but is in fact a getter. The breaking through of an instinctive parsimony usually betrays her.

In spite of her dependence on others and her susceptibility to suggestions, she stubbornly insists on carrying through her resolutions. She is extremely self-centred, bombastically spreading her ego, but by switching on her charm she manages to hide her lack of social interest.

Mrs. W. has the philosophy of the escapist, who takes refuge in inventive imagination, and in spite of her materialistic outlook on life she is inclined to build castles in the air. In conclusion it must be pointed out that the writer is neither physically nor morally strong, lacks firmness of character and is loosely principled. It appears as if she never submitted to intelligent discipline and will therefore never be able to adapt herself to adverse circumstances.

In reply to this analysis the Educational Authority replied, 'Everybody concerned on the case thought the report remarkably apposite,' and in response to a request supplied Mrs. W.'s full case history and a note which said that in a Parental Attitude test given to her, Mrs. W. had a score for non-detachment heavily weighted on the side of Suppression rather than of Protection. Her score for Unconcern on the detached side was rather high also, which at first glance would appear inconsistent. 'Where there is a pronounced score for both Suppression and Unconcern,' said the note, 'the attitude appears to be that of rejection of the children i.e. preventing them from being a nuisance when present (suppression) and forgetting them when they are out of sight (unconcern). Both children have been sent away on our advice.'

A copy of the report of the psychiatrist at the local Mental Hospital was enclosed and is given here in detail:

Mrs. W. (widow) aged 47.

Informant patient only; no relative within reach.

Reason for Referral: Personality Difficulties. Cannot get on with other people. Feels that everyone is out to do her down and feels that everything that does not suit her is deliberate persecution and injury. Cannot keep a job. Had a nervous breakdown two years ago and was without work for twelve months. Has had three positions since then, complains that she still cannot concentrate as she ought to do. Has fears (admitted with reluctance) of losing her mental balance.

Her two children are under treatment in this department, and appear to be suffering from their mother's lack of stability. In view of this and of her own family history, it would seem desirable for her to be under psychiatric observation.

Family History.

Father died of cancer when patient was six.

Mother deteriorated from the time of her husband's death. Became hallucinated and full of delusions. Was two or three times in Mental Hospital. Admitted for the last time when patient was fourteen and died in hospital.

Maternal Aunt: was liable to puerperal psychosis. Has nine children and was admitted to Mental Hospital on each occasion.

Sibling. (Patient).

Sister: Unmarried. Works in Government Office. Gives occasional financial help for specific purposes e.g. is now paying fees for patient's daughter at a Commercial School.

Three others died in childhood.

Personal History.

Childhood: Born in a Midland town. After father's death returned to mother's home. Has memories of hiding from her mother for days at a time; on one occasion banging the door to occupy the mother's attention so that the younger sister could escape. When her mother was for the last time taken to hospital, the two children lived by themselves for some time, eating stores and garden produce, till it came to the notice of the authorities and they were taken to the Workhouse. (Mrs. W. is still resentful of this and has 'never forgiven them'.) Later she was placed in the home of an ex-bargee of whom she became very fond.

Menstruation.

Menstruated for the first time while in the Workhouse without previous knowledge or warning. From then until the birth of her first child she suffered acute incapacitating pain with each period, not relieved until she had vomited.

Education.

Had been attending the High School until admitted to the Workhouse. On her return she felt incapable of explaining her absence, was called stubborn, and that was the end of her schooling. Later she took the normal school exams by correspondence, qualifying as an uncertificated teacher.

Employment.

During the war 1914-1918 she worked as a clerk in an Army Department in a small town. Made a friend there who was going through a training college and under her influence decided to become a teacher. Was a supplementary teacher in a village school while taking her correspondence course, then became head of the village school (1922-24). Was happy there, but never seems to have been happy in her work since. After her husband's death she returned to teaching, at first in a mixed school (1935-38). Was unhappy there, felt persecuted, ignored and ill-treated, and was finally discharged. Was probably quite impossible to work with. Then went to another village school, where the persecution continued. She broke down, and before she was really well took a job as a clerk. Broke down again and was then without work for eighteen months. In October 1941 she got a job in a chain store. Threw it up in May 1942. Went as a clerk to an Engineering Company. The Manager obtained permission to dismiss her in August, but she is at present working as a clerk again.

Marriage.

Married in 1924 a farm labourer in the village where she taught. Was happy at first, felt that she had at last found someone to whom she could open freely. Now tends to feel that happiness was an illusion, as the later years were ones of friction and estrangement. She hoped that she would assist her husband to become independent, but he showed no desire for it, disapproved of her wish to get work outside the house and compared her home-making abilities unfavourably with his mother's. She feels that he was always dominated by his mother. He died after about ten years of marriage following a move from a County Hospital to London, for which Mrs. W. bitterly blames the hospital authorities.

Children.

A boy died at $8\frac{1}{2}$ months.

A boy died at birth.

A daughter, born 24.4.30 I.Q. 105, Terman-Merrill. A very immature, restless, nervous child, afraid of failure but anxious to be in the limelight and achieving her desire by troublesome behaviour. Against advice her mother placed her in a Commercial College.

A second daughter born 11.11.32. I.Q. 121 Terman-Merrill. Attended school, a more active go-ahead child than the older sister. She sought satisfaction in petty pilfering. Mrs. W. wanted none of the elder children. When the first daughter was a baby, she remembered having an almost irresistible impulse to draw a knife across the child's throat. The younger is the only one for whom she has ever had any maternal affection.

Present Home Conditions.

123

A very poor slovenly home, even by the lowest standards. The place is littered, untidy and dirty. Mrs. W. seems to lack mental energy even to begin making a home. She keeps innumerable cats and kittens, all appearing more or less neglected, and has been in trouble with the authorities for an attempt to keep goats.

No further comments seem to be needed in face of this fully reported case. In the light of this report undoubtedly the children had to be entrusted to the authorities.

CHAPTER NINE

Handwritings and Drawings of Deaf Children

Deaf children do not necessarily lack intelligence, but their handicap does hamper their development particularly in infancy, so that they are not able to express themselves at as early an age as normal children. They begin coherent thinking after gaining experience through lip-reading, but since speech presents difficulties these children often enjoy the opportunity of conveying their thoughts in paintings. These pictures are generally uncommonly rich in colour and bold in design. One of the most striking and at the same time pathetic features of deaf children's paintings is the treatment of the mouth which in almost every case is accentuated in size and colour.

In this chapter the writings and pictures of ten deaf children are discussed. The children's ages range from nine to twelve years. Each script and each picture has been graphologically examined, the same rules being applied for both drawings and writings. The characteristics of these children as shown in their drawings and scripts are checked by remarks from their headmaster. The teachers of these deaf children take a very special interest in their charges, so that each child is favoured with individual guidance.

The children were supplied with large sheets of drawing paper covered with all sorts of lines and criss-cross designs and were asked from these lines and criss-cross designs to evolve their own pictures. This is now a widely-used method of getting children to draw.[1] From the artist's point of view the rhythm and composition of the scribbled lines run through the finished work and give a more pleasing effect than a copy of any picture laboriously produced. From the psychologist's point of view this kind of drawing is revealing. The child finds inspiration in the scribbles and projects on to the paper images from his unconscious mind.

Figure 92 shows the work of Anthony, aged 11, who is congenitally partially deaf. He describes his drawing in these words: 'The spider is touching the lady's hair. The man is smoking the cigarette.

---

1   See *Child Art to Man Art* by William Johnstone.

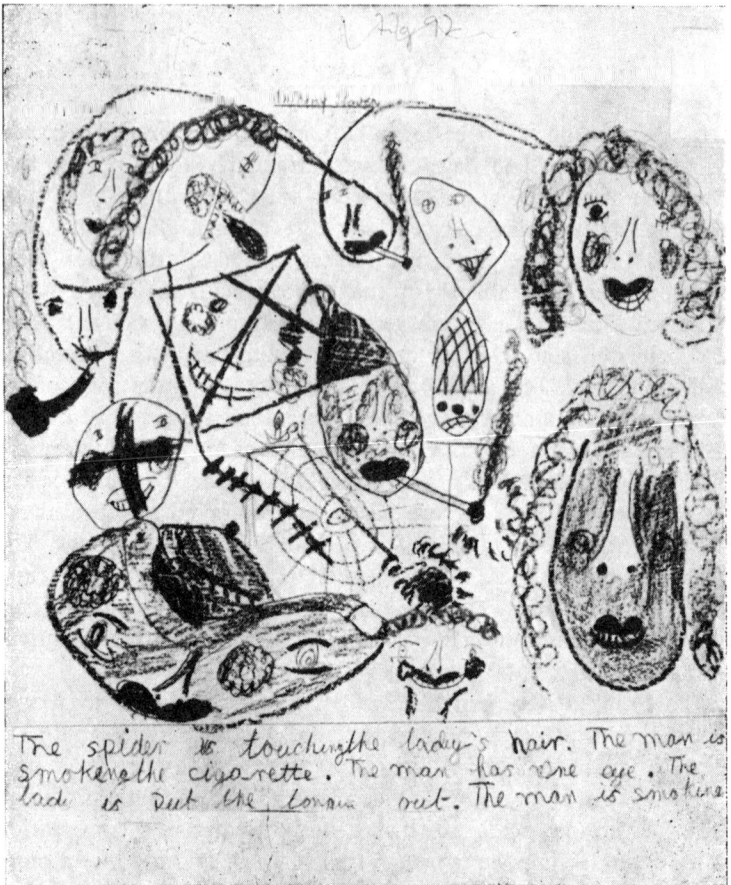

FIG. 92 (reduced)

The man has one eye. The lady puts the tongue out, the man is smoking his pipe. The lady is falling off the table. The man is listening to the wireless.'

The accentuation of the mouth is particularly striking, for the mouth is the organ which the boy has to observe as a means of communication. The fact that the man in the middle of the drawing has only one eye may be interpreted as a compensation for Anthony's own organ inferiority, a consolation to ameliorate his attitude towards his deficient hearing.

It is impossible to detect a table or a lady falling off it, nor is there a man listening to the wireless. These pictures are obviously only in Anthony's mind and have not found expression on paper.

Anthony has a good idea of a simplified technique for drawing noses. Two lines and two dots each suffice, yet he manages in each case to express an individual nose, which is extremely clever and resourceful of him.

Many stirring thoughts seem to be in this boy's mind: evidently there is no dull moment. The boldness of the drawing testifies to Anthony's daring, his readiness to come into the open unreservedly and reveal his thoughts.

There is a striking formation in the lower left corner of the drawing, the head of a woman with red cheeks, two eyes, a nose and a large red mouth. She is a red-haired lady wearing a brown cap, and her nose and mouth show a bird-like form. It is a weird and fanciful picture.

In the top left corner a man smokes a pipe. Towering over him is another man, joined with two more heads. The lady in profile puts out her tongue and another smokes a cigarette. A kite, a spider, a spider's web, a candle and a candlestick are included in an over-all design. The inventive originality of the boy is really amazing. Much conflict is being expressed in this whirl and turmoil. Anthony is erratic in his reactions but definitely shows an artistic temperament, and although his thoughts are somewhat incoherent he is clever in associative thinking. Life is full of surprises for him, but he is not always as cheerful as the vivid colouring of his painting suggests.

Anthony's handwriting (Fig. 92a), when compared with his picture leads in part to the same conclusions, but also shows a different facet of his personality. It shows a boy with a lively imagination, a clever boy but troublesome. He is bizarre in his reactions. Some of his letter-forms are ingenious and the pressure, the direction and the size of the writing are rather irregular so that we cannot tell

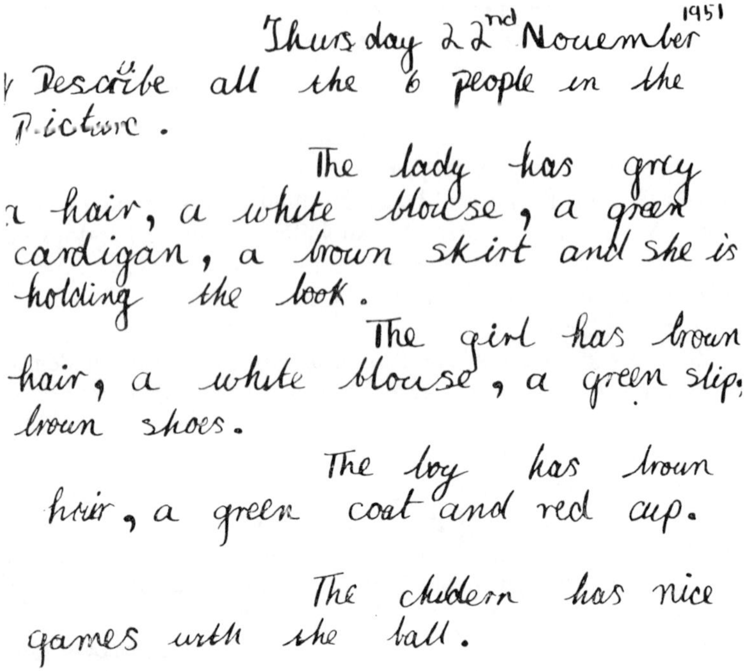

Thursday 22nd November 1951

Describe all the 6 people in the Picture.

The lady has grey hair, a white blouse, a green cardigan, a brown skirt and she is holding the book.

The girl has brown hair, a white blouse, a green slip, brown shoes.

The boy has brown hair, a green coat and red cap.

The children has nice games with the ball.

FIG. 92a (reduced)

what to expect next. The plasticity of his writing is, however, outstanding. Light and shade are equally distributed and speak for a progressive adaptation and the ability to express himself lucidly.

Anthony is a conscientious boy and works well at school being full of energy and vivacious activity. He is a man in the making and sex problems seem to occupy his mind unduly. He is an excellent observer but very critical, even sharp and aggressive at times. Some resentment related to his handicap can be detected in the fine end-strokes which are pointed and directed towards his fellow-beings. He can be defiant and is given to sudden tempers when least expected. This boy has a concrete mind and an objective attitude to life more pronounced than usual in those of his age. He has a quick and versatile comprehension and his logic is sound, assets which are of special value to a deaf child.

Although Anthony's handwriting shows productivity, it does not suggest an artistic bent. A sense of space, a good sense of proportion and an even distribution of light and shade show, rather, a gift for draughtsmanship.

NOTE.—The capital 'T's' in the word 'The' at the beginning of every paragraph show an upward-striving tendency and at the same time demonstrate a good intelligence, but the capital 'T' in the date (line 1) is significantly shaped quite differently from those in the text. The diverse styles in which Anthony expresses himself suggest a moody disposition but at the same time a versatile personality.

The head master's comment was: 'I agree with every word of your study of Anthony. Briefly my own description would be: superficially likeable, receptive, reasonably intelligent, but character spoilt by a bad temper and unpleasant interest in sexual affairs.'

FIG. 93 (reduced)

Figure 93 shows the work of Donald, aged 11 years 2 months, who is slightly deaf. A marked proneness to morbidity is expressed in Donald's drawing which he explains in these words: 'The two murderers are eating the people in the house. The spider is climbing up the body.'

What a ghastly fantasy! Blood is oozing out of the head of one figure and blood flows from the body of the man on the left who has been pierced with a dagger. This horrible picture suggests immediately that it is the painting of a boy whose mentality has been coloured by a traumatic experience.

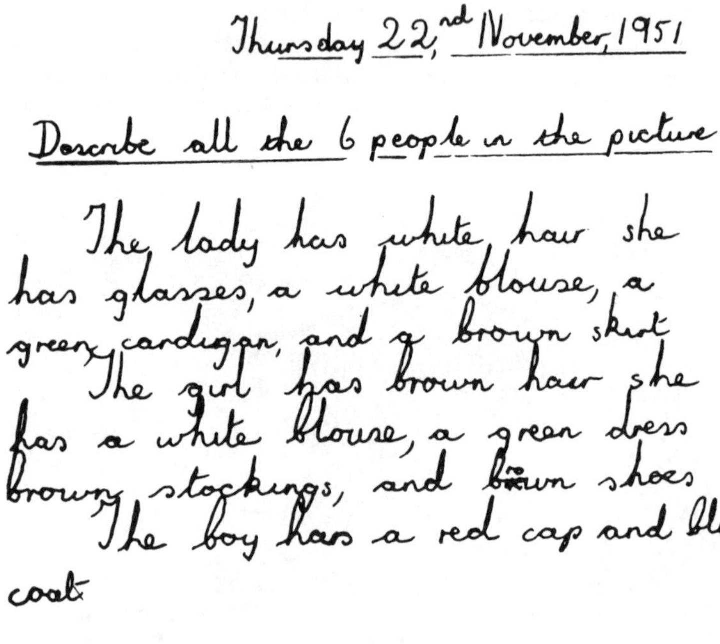

Thursday 22nd November, 1951

Describe all the 6 people in the picture

The lady has white hair she has glasses, a white blouse, a green cardigan, and a brown skirt
The girl has brown hair she has a white blouse, a green dress brown stockings, and brown shoes
The boy has a red cap and blue coat

D.

FIG. 93a (reduced)

Donald's handwriting (Fig. 93a) reveals that he is a very ambitious boy whose main interests are intellectual. Emotions are sacrificed for the sake of success. Striving upwards is praiseworthy except when it is carried too far: when overdone it can become a negative attribute. This boy has no intellectual background and therefore often gets muddled because of his interests and ambitions. He shows great manual dexterity but lacks clarity in thinking. Great anxiety and peculiar reactions can be detected in his handwriting. He is morally and physically weak and tries to compensate for it by mental ability. He has an hysterical urge for ostentation combined with an inner emptiness. It is because he is emotionally inhibited and frustrated that he seizes every opportunity to outwit his fellow-beings, and his anxiety and neurotic fears lead him at times to definitely untruthful statements.

Donald is productive as well as receptive, but on the whole he gives most of his attention to gaining external effects.

If we compare this boy's drawing with his writing we find that the drawing expresses primitive urges while the writing shows quite different traits—ambition, anxiety and frustration. In the drawing the table is laid to show cannibalism: there are knives and forks, a teacup, and the human bones that are to be devoured by the murderers. The writing on the other hand shows fear. The difference between Donald's artistic efforts and his scholarly achievements almost suggests a dual personality.

The headmaster's comment was: 'This is a very accurate description. Your opinion of a traumatic experience is confirmed by other symptoms. He is an extremely likeable boy with a great urge to get on. He is very practical and inventive. He sometimes shows unreasonable fears.'

Figure 94 shows the work of Alice, aged 11 years 4 months, who is congenitally partially deaf. Alice's own description of her painting says, 'The man has a black beard and dirty hands. He never washes his hands and he likes to drink dirty water. The black nail was on the chair, and if the man sits on the nail he will hurt himself and the nail will stick in the man.'

Though quite incomprehensible in parts, some of this picture is very amusing. The nail, which is the smallest thing in the picture is made significant by its clever arrangement. The man smiles broadly: so far he has not been hurt. As in many a lively cartoon

the joke resides in what will happen when certain inevitable contacts are made. Alice has no sadistic tendencies: it just tickles her
to think that the man may sit on the nail. The clock on his lap is
significant of time, which must play an important part in Alice's

FIG. 94 (reduced)

life. The two phallic symbols near the man's head may be meant to
represent his ears. Perhaps he is listening for an alarm bell at
twelve, which is often the hour of decisive movement in story and
in school life.

The mouths of all the figures in the picture are accentuated by
vivid colours or protruding teeth. The red lips of the head situated
in the right hand corner extend as far as the handle of the teacup.

132

The background is blue like the sea, but a brown object held up by the middle figure cannot be identified. Alice seems to lack a sense of proportion and is not very explicit in conveying her meaning.

Alice's handwriting was unfortunately done with a ball-pen which makes it difficult to examine, but there is no doubt that the girl is severely inhibited and secretive. She is far from truthful, a condition caused by lack of security and a sense of guilt. Her script is full of corrections which show that she is striving all the time to 'make good' and wipe out her self-reproaches. These reproaches may be caused only by her own fantasies, but the corrections help to restore her self-confidence. Whenever she embarks on a new task Alice feels intensely insecure.

This child's writing (Fig. 94a) suggests that she comes from a home of discord and strife, and that her consequent moodiness and irritability drive her disharmoniously in all directions. The slovenliness of her ways suggests a topsy-turvy background where cleanliness and order are missing.

A competitive striving for intellectual superiority is apparent in Alice's writing. In some of her reactions she is obviously quick and she has a very good idea of how best to avail herself of the space at her disposal. The child is highly strung, sensitive and insecure and she has great difficulty in expressing herself because her emotions are inhibited. Her intellectual capacity is only mediocre, but she works hard and strives to outdo her companions, and she accommodates herself to the frustration and non-fulfilment which are due to her dependent spirit. She is not very receptive or productive, a fact testified also by her artistic efforts, and her reactions are irregular because of her morbid mind and vague fears.

Alice's drawing and her writing are not identical in value. They appear to originate from two different levels, the emotional and the intellectual, and to show two different cross-sections of her personality.

The headmaster's comment was: 'A very accurate reading of her character. She does lack confidence in tackling new jobs and processes. Her supreme efforts to make good have had considerable results and by hard slogging alone she is able to keep abreast of other girls superior in intelligence and opportunities. Her greatest drawback is her sensitivity and her distrust of all adults.'

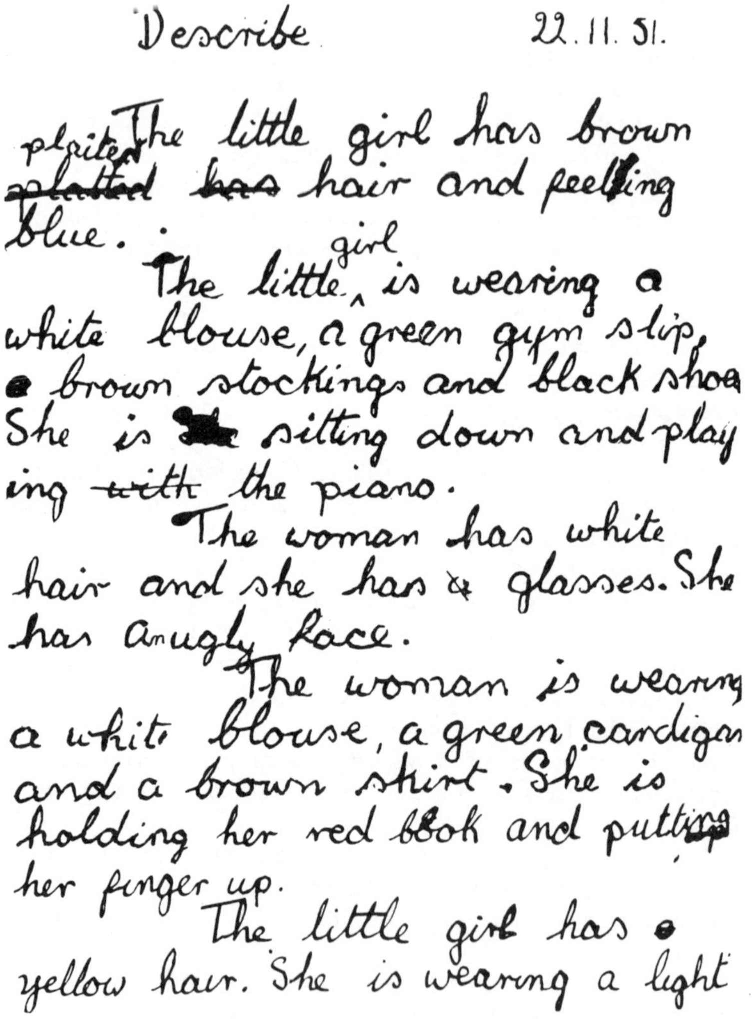

Describe.   22. 11. 51.

~~plaite~~ The little girl has brown ~~platted~~ ~~has~~ hair and peeling blue. .

The little girl, is wearing a white blouse, a green gym slip, a brown stockings and black shoe She is ~~the~~ sitting down and play ing ~~with~~ the piano.

The woman has white hair and she has & glasses. She has a ugly face.

The woman is wearing a white blouse, a green cardigan and a brown skirt. She is holding her red book and putting her finger up.

The little girl has a yellow hair. She is wearing a light

FIG. 94a (reduced)

134

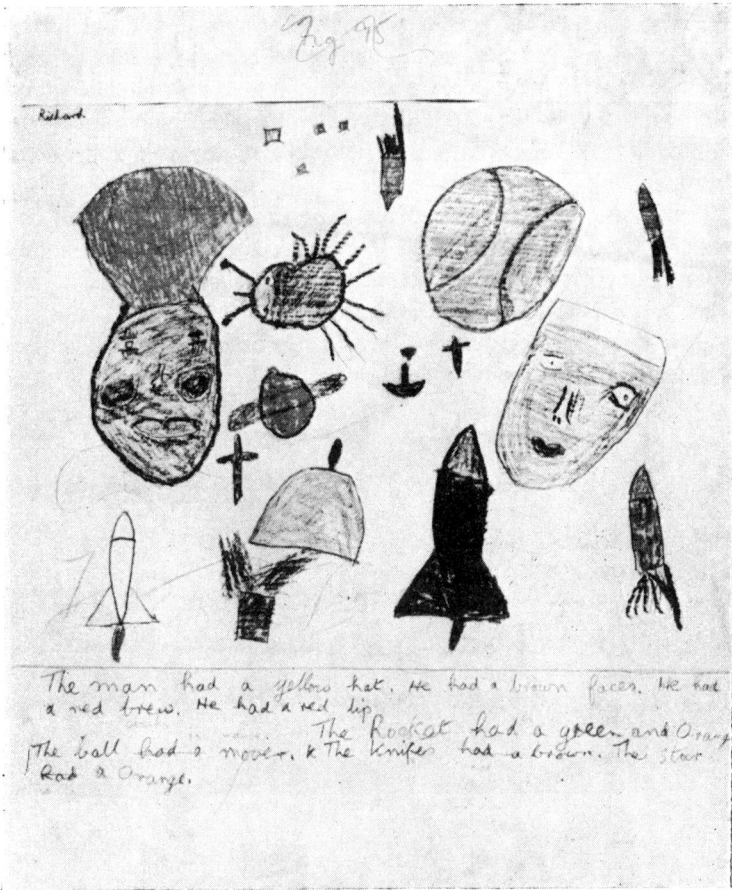

FIG. 95 (reduced)

Figure 95 shows the work of Richard, aged 11 years 9 months, who is congenitally severely deaf. Richard's own description of his picture says, 'The man had a yellow hat. He had a brown face, he had red cheeks, he had red lips. The rocket is green and orange, the ball is mauve. The knives are brown. The star is orange.'

It is by means of Richard's description that we realize what the

135

drawing should actually represent. Lips are again emphasized, and note also the two daggers which suddenly appear without fitting into the design, and the three penknives, a big one, a smaller one, and one that is incomplete and upside-down, instruments which give testimony to the boy's destructive moods which are by no means harmless. Richard is troublesome and excitable and on the defensive.

The burning candle has no justification in the picture and one wonders what the boy is trying to convey. The ball and the rocket are well-conceived and vividly coloured. The orange stars do not seem to have any special significance.

How does this conglomeration of faces and all sorts of articles compare with the handwriting?

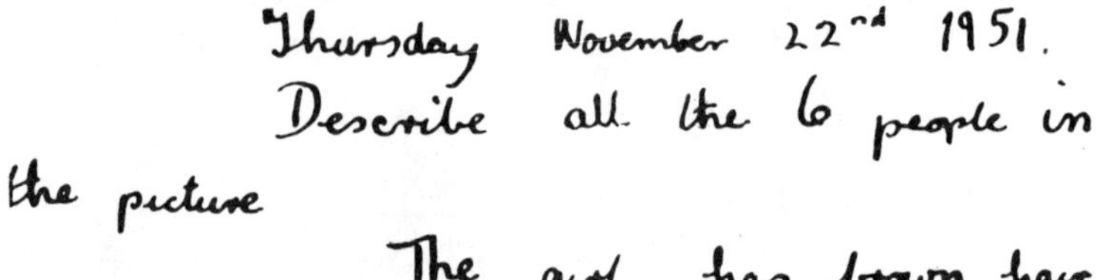

> Thursday November 22nd 1951.
> Describe all the 6 people in the picture
>
> The girl has brown hair a white blouse, a green slip, brown stockings, brown shoes, she is playing the piano
>
> The boy has brown hair, a red cap, a brown shirt and he is shouting to Mother
>
> The lady has white hair, a brown face

FIG. 95a (reduced)

The writing (Fig. 95a) is orderly and well fitted into the space. Richard is seen to be sincere and frank. He seems a precocious child, particularly if we take into consideration his handicap which excludes an early development. He has a great deal of energy and tenacity at his disposal, but he sometimes uses them wrongly.

All details are meticulously observed by Richard and he is able to give his thoughts a plastic expression worthy of an older boy. He is diligent, conscientious and painstaking. He tries to eliminate his subjective point of view and has the gift of concentrating on his actions. He is a lonely child who does not make friends easily. Although receptive and quick in the uptake, he does not seem to be particularly productive.

Richard's drawing is immature and without any logical meaning, yet his handwriting is the product of a gifted boy. These two things are irreconcilable as the expression of the same personality.

The headmaster's comment was: 'Very accurate findings. He is sincere and frank, but very troublesome and nervy. As term goes on, he gets more and more naughty, but everyone has a soft spot for him all the same. He is conscientious and painstaking as long as his interest holds. He is also a very affectionate child'.

Figure 96 shows the work of Bertha, aged 12 years 1 month, who is congenitally very deaf. The description of Bertha's picture says, 'The lady is holding the teapot. The boy is holding the fork and the knife for the food. The lady is sitting down in the chair. The boy does not like the food. The lady is making the boy eat his food.' (Some words have to be supplied in Bertha's description.)

By means of the expression of the mouth with its teeth showing Bertha indicates the lady's firm determination that the boy shall eat his food. Similarly the tight-lipped mouth of the boy shows that he has made up his mind to resist her command. He looks most provocative and it is interesting to wonder who will have to give in at the end of the argument. It is amazing how Bertha can express so much by so little. She knows how to use her space well.

In her handwriting (Fig. 96a) neither conflict nor resistance can be discerned. Bertha appears to be accommodating to a certain extent, yet we can observe in her writing the same determination and obstinacy as she wanted to show in her picture. She must have the last word and, although rather primitive and stolid, usually gains her point. She is not excitable, but is not inclined to give way once her mind is made up. She is slow in the uptake and her rhythm is retarded.

FIG. 96 (reduced)

Having had an upbringing remarkably free from fear, Bertha is neither frustrated nor inhibited. She is not very easy to cope with for she is undoubtedly a pampered child, but she is a warm-hearted girl who likes to mix with others so long as they do not attempt to thwart her. She has accepted her handicap without bitterness or resentment.

The headmaster's comment was, 'Very accurate findings. She is stolid, easygoing and very slow on the uptake. She has been

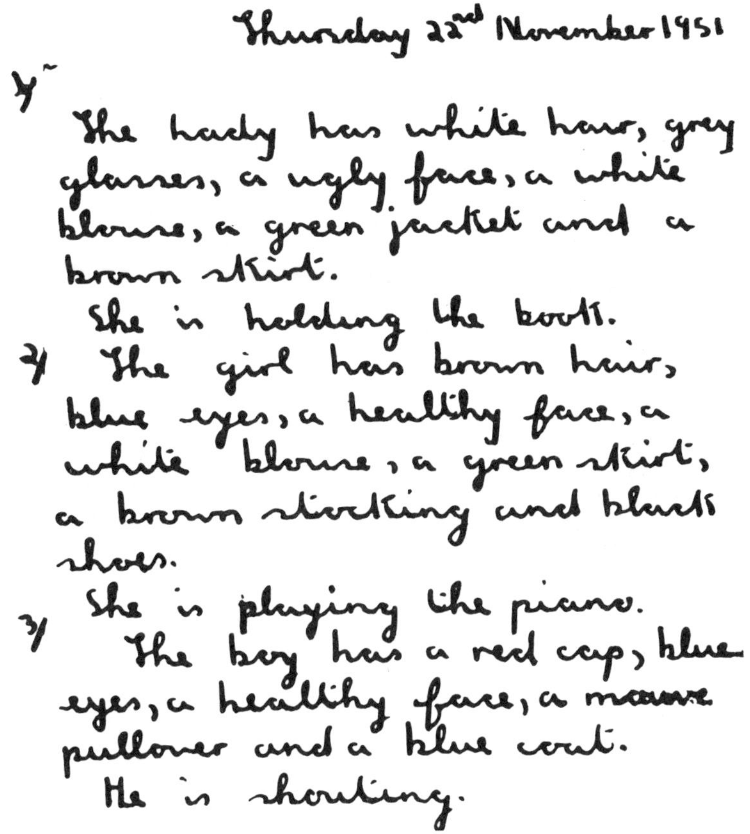

Thursday 22nd November 1951

The lady has white hair, grey glasses, a ugly face, a white blouse, a green jacket and a brown skirt.

She is holding the book.

The girl has brown hair, blue eyes, a healthy face, a white blouse, a green skirt, a brown stocking and black shoes.

She is playing the piano.

The boy has a red cap, blue eyes, a healthy face, a mauve pullover and a blue coat.

He is shouting.

FIG. 96a (reduced)

pampered and is very backward indeed, although bucking up considerably at the moment.'

Figure 97 shows the work of Lilian, aged 11 years 11 months, who is congenitally partially deaf. The description of her painting says, 'Mother is holding the baby with big girl for a walk. Cat saw lady and baby, cat like baby-girl.'

The drawing, in which the cat is comparatively the best part, is immature and childish, showing that Lilian's development is definitely retarded. She seems to be in a muddle, and the wondering

FIG. 97 (reduced)

eyes of the big girl may well portray her complexities. The mother, carrying a handbag, has a fierce expression, the baby is round faced and chubby, but the big girl has a very sad expression and looks as perplexed as if she were wondering what life is all about.

The emphasized mouths of the three figures in the picture are remarkable, especially if we compare them with the insignificant proportions of the noses. Ears are non-existent or covered by the hair. The cat's ears are outstanding. Lucky cat, she can hear! The sky is studded with stars but at the same time the sun appears in the right hand corner, an inconsistency which does not bother the artist. The sky and stars are blue, the sun golden yellow.

There are some sharp and aggressive strokes apparent in Lilian's handwriting (Fig. 97a) and outbursts of temper and tantrum-reactions can be graphologically observed. The girl seems to live

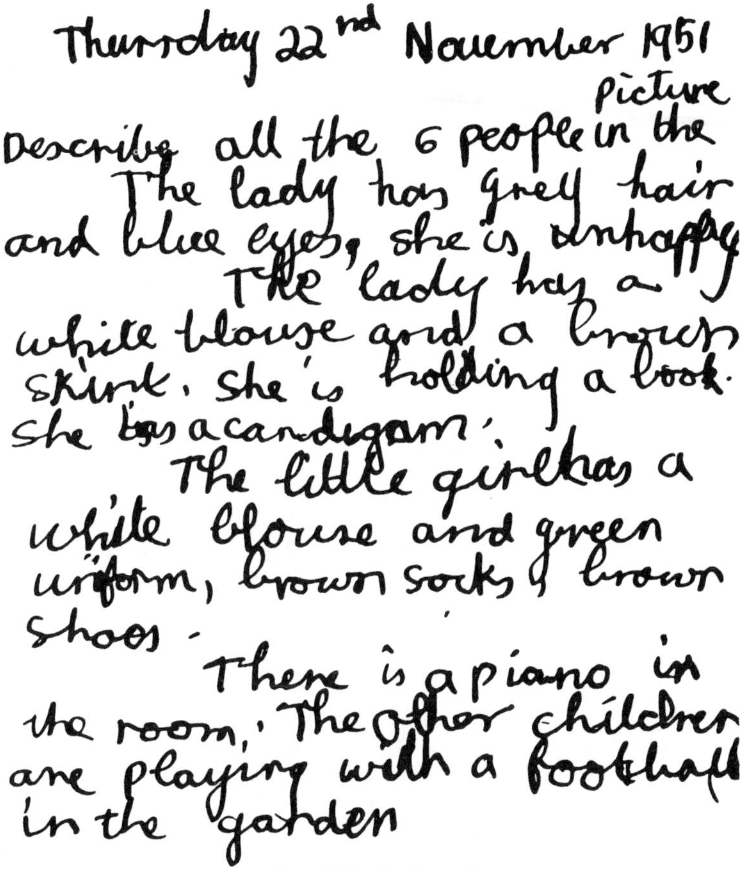

Thursday 22nd November 1951
Describe all the 6 people in the picture
The lady has grey hair and blue eyes, she is unhappy
The lady has a white blouse and a brown skirt. She is holding a book. She has a cardigam.
The little girl has a white blouse and green uniform, brown socks & brown shoes.
There is a piano in the room. The other children are playing with a football in the garden

FIG. 97a (reduced)

in a state of tension as can be seen from the strong pressure, while the many retracements and corrections give evidence of conflicts

141

within herself. Nevertheless she is a girl of kind disposition, talkative and inquisitive even if rather muddled and inconsistent.

In spite of a marked instability Lilian keeps up the paragraphs, a fact which shows another contradition in her character. She is obviously very excitable and needs careful handling. Being a bad mixer she has difficulty in making friends. Her poor intelligence cannot possibly lead her to logical conclusions, and her moods are changeable being either too boisterous or too helpless. She is the extravert type who likes to show off. Nervous stress and inhibitions alternate with a lack of control in Lilian, and these states are evidently caused by conflict and disharmony in her home-conditions, but these disturbing factors are beyond the child's control.

The headmaster's comment was, 'A very good all round description.'

FIG. 98 (reduced)

Figure 98 shows the work of Laura, aged 10 years, who is

congenitally severely deaf. The explanation of her picture reads, 'Mother said be good, then daddy will buy fireworks.'

The interior of the home is excellently rendered. The most outstanding feature is a vividly coloured carpet, but there are many other good points. The fireplace has a blazing fire, there is a picture on the wall, an electric pendant hangs from the ceiling, the window is curtained and the door open. The wallpaper has a spotted pattern and the floor boards are well polished. The picture in fact portrays a homely peaceful atmosphere to which Laura is longing to return. Tension is absent for there is no threat of punishment, that negative educational measure, but instead the positive element is stressed: 'You must be good, then daddy will buy you fireworks.'

Laura is diligent and conscientious and her handwriting shows

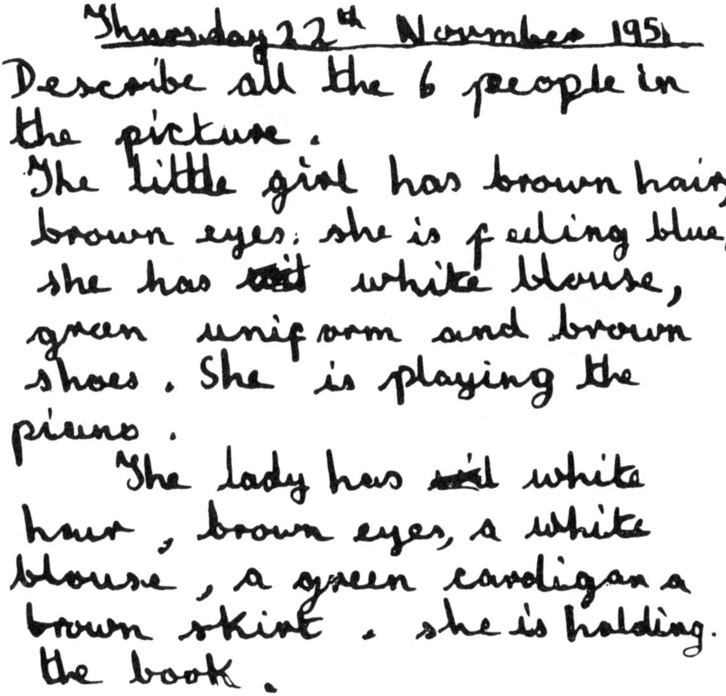

> Thursday 22ᵗʰ November 1951
> Describe all the 6 people in the picture.
> The little girl has brown hair, brown eyes; she is feeling blue, she has a white blouse, green uniform and brown shoes. She is playing the piano.
>   The lady has white hair, brown eyes, a white blouse, a green cardigan a brown skirt. she is holding the book.

FIG. 98a (reduced)

manual dexterity (Fig. 98a). Some of her letter-formations are
mature, as if produced by an older child. This maturity is not however maintained throughout the script for Laura also produces some
infantile formations. The general result of her efforts is a worth-
while achievement.

Visual impressions go deep with Laura, but she is more painstaking than original. She sets out with great confidence on a task
but during the process of her work she sometimes loses faith in her
abilities. She usually manages to succeed in the end, but an excessive eagerness to please causes uneasiness and may even make her
deceitful.

Laura's impediment makes her withdraw from other children.
Apparently she has chosen the neurotic solution to her problem.

FIG. 99 (reduced)

144

She is, however, trying hard to accommodate herself to limited fulfilment.

In spite of favourable home conditions Laura is a rigid and highly strung child who is even sulky at times, and these facts make it rather difficult to cope with her.

The headmaster's comment was, 'Also a very good all-round description. She has a very good home indeed. Not a wealthy one, but one that gives love and security.'

Figure 99 shows the work of Lena, aged 9 years 11 months, who is severely deaf as the result of meningitis at the age of 2. Lena's description of her picture says, 'Mother is reading the newspaper, the baby is very happy because he is playing with the ball. Mother said, "Outside afterwards for the fireworks".'

The theme of the picture is similar to that of Figure 98, but Lena cannot express herself nearly so well as Laura, for she suffers from a psycho-somatic condition due to meningitis and this has to be taken into consideration.

We see the interior of her home, an electric fire switched on, a rug on the floor, a picture on the wall, but the scene is incomplete compared with Laura's.

The mother's mouth which Lena seems to observe for instructions stands out prominently. According to the girl her mother takes life easily for she sits down and reads the paper, while the baby who has a rather unhappy expression, is playing with the ball.

Lena's handwriting (Fig. 99a) reveals a rather cramped and constrained disposition. She is a girl of many moods but practises intense external composure. Whenever her self-discipline flags she gets excitable and peevish. In spite of a shy manner she likes to be in the limelight and is an excellent actress—in fact her behaviour is full of contradictions. Her charming and fascinating approach makes her a general favourite, and this satisfies her competitive urge to be attractive, an ambition for which she is prepared to sacrifice a great deal.

Being highly impressionable Lena is sensitive and susceptible to praise and rebukes and this leads to a nervy irritability and an impetuous expression of emotion. Innately she is very kind-hearted and accommodating but she can be quick to anger when rubbed up the wrong way. She tries hard to conquer her temper, not an easy task when her impulsive nature is taken into consideration. She is always grateful and appreciative of any kind of affection extended to her.

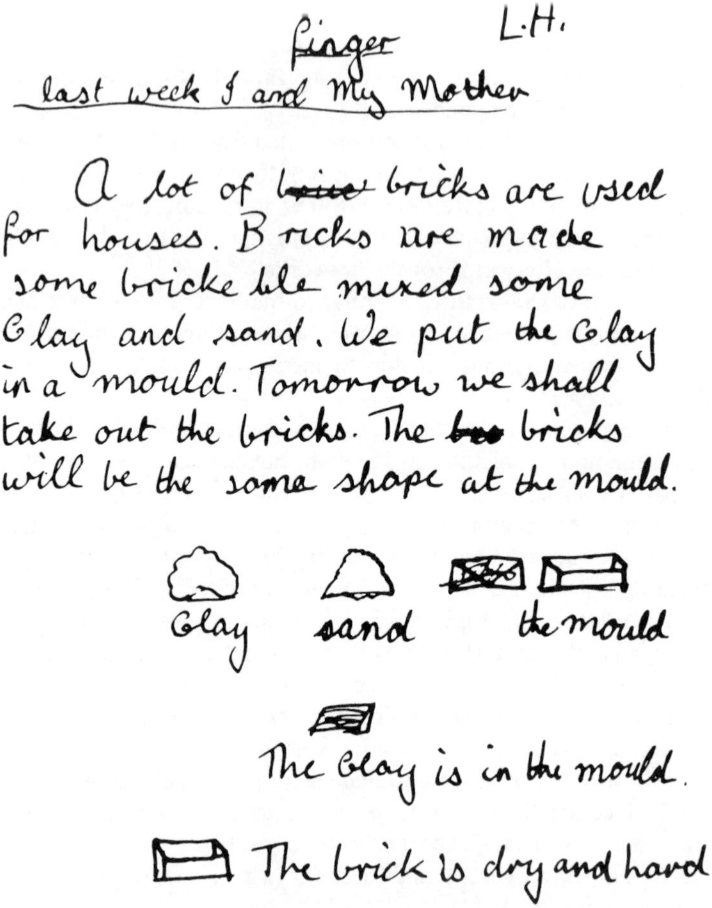

finger   L.H.

last week I and My Mother

A lot of ~~brick~~ bricks are used for houses. Bricks are made some bricke ble mixed some Clay and sand. We put the Clay in a mould. Tomorrow we shall take out the bricks. The ~~two~~ bricks will be the same shape at the mould.

Clay   sand   the mould

The Clay is in the mould.

The brick is dry and hard

FIG. 99a (reduced)

Although of great intellectual vivacity Lena appears to be dazed at times. This is in all probability a residue of illness, for physically she appears to be strong.

146

This girl is industrious, embarks on her duties with a certain flair and with innate energy and is perfectly capable of taking the initiative. Her rhythm is fast, and she works well and quickly. As a matter of fact she is too hasty at times, and this leads to omissions in an otherwise conscientiously carried through task. Her logic is sound and her arguments are brought forward with remarkable determination. She is socially minded and she reacts in a natural way to all situations. Although her work of art reveals no imagination her handwriting shows symptoms of fantasy.

Lena has a very complicated character and there is more conflict within her than can be detected on the surface. In spite of her moody disposition she has a very reliable character. There is an observable discrepancy between her precocity and her immaturity. She has a quick judgment far above her years. Her mentality is really perplexing for some of her repressed affects come to the fore in awkward situations particularly in her intimate family circle.

The headmaster's comment was, 'I have studied your report on Lena and quite agree with you. Her previous teacher, who knows her better than I, says that you have hit the nail on the head, especially regarding her practising intense external composure in spite of varying moods.'

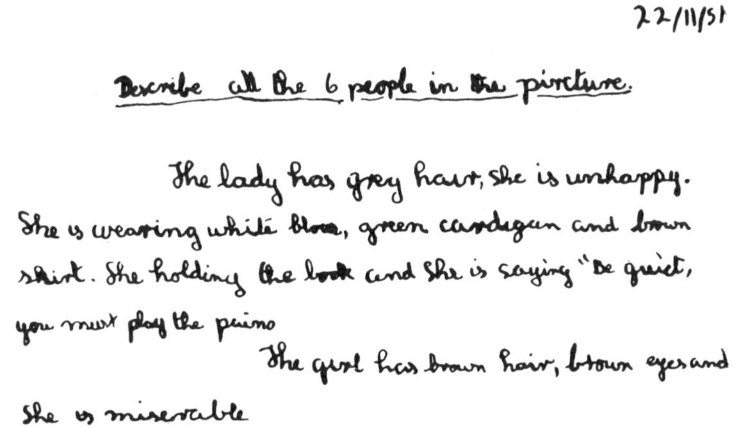

22/11/51

Describe all the 6 people in the picture.

The lady has grey hair, she is unhappy. She is wearing white blouse, green cardigan and brown shirt. She holding the book and she is saying "Be quiet, you must play the piano

The girl has brown hair, brown eyes and she is miserable

FIG. 100 (reduced)

Figure 100 shows the work of Ian, aged 9 years 4 months, who is

147

congenitally severely deaf. No drawing was available so his hand-writing alone is analysed here. Ian's writing reveals a cramped frustrated boy who has great difficulty in expressing himself. The writing is narrow and laboured as well as small. It shows twisted formations which suggest a twisted mentality while the loops of the letters y, g, and q are very short and indicate a weak central nervous system. Some of the connections, for example those in the word 'she' (line 3), show a great deal of tension.

Though usually he is constrained and artificial, Ian has some clever reactions. He is receptively gifted and methodical in his work, and being endowed with an even temperament he is able to accept his deficient hearing unflinchingly. His achievements are patchy but he works with great concentration. He has many difficulties within himself to solve.

Ian's writing shows remarkable maturity. The boy is a very slow worker owing to ill health, but he is trying hard to succeed.

The headmaster's comment was, 'Very accurate findings. A very intelligent boy for his age, in fact too intelligent for his limited means of expression. Excessively excitable and an extreme introvert. He comes from a totally deaf family therefore his attitude to com-munication is a preference for manual signs and finger spelling rather than lip-reading and speech. He is now severely ill, which you have apparently foreseen.'

Figure 101 shows the work of Josephine, aged 11 years 4 months, who is congenitally partially deaf. Her description of the drawing says, 'The man is fighting with the other man. The man's nose is bleeding. The man's wife is very happy, because he won the fight.'

The lively colours and individual character of the design in this picture suggest a lively mind and an independent spirit. In this vivacious and expressive work we see a sanguine temperament, amazingly clear logic, quick judgment and intelligent observation. The feeling for form and movement is well expressed. Note the enjoyment of those who watch the fight. The man in the left hand corner shows his enjoyment in a broad smile that shows his teeth. The boxer's wife on the left is extremely happy and obviously proud of her husband's victory. Even without Josephine's explanation we can interpret this expressive smile. The boxer looks self-satisfied at having succeeded, while the nose of the poor vanquished man is bleeding and his downcast attitude leaves no doubt about his defeat.

FIG. 101 (reduced)

We note again three accentuated mouths which are very expressive.

Josephine is a versatile, diligent and strong girl, whose handwriting (Fig. 101a) suggests a productively gifted personality endowed with a lively spirit. She is vivacious in every respect, has a keen imagination, lucidity of mind and an independent nature. She shows tenacity of purpose and her work is carried through with intense concentration and thoroughness. Some of the retracements in her handwriting, for example in the word 'miserable' (line 6) might suggest that Josephine is troubled with a sense of guilt which she is trying to discard, but she actually comes from a happy background.

149

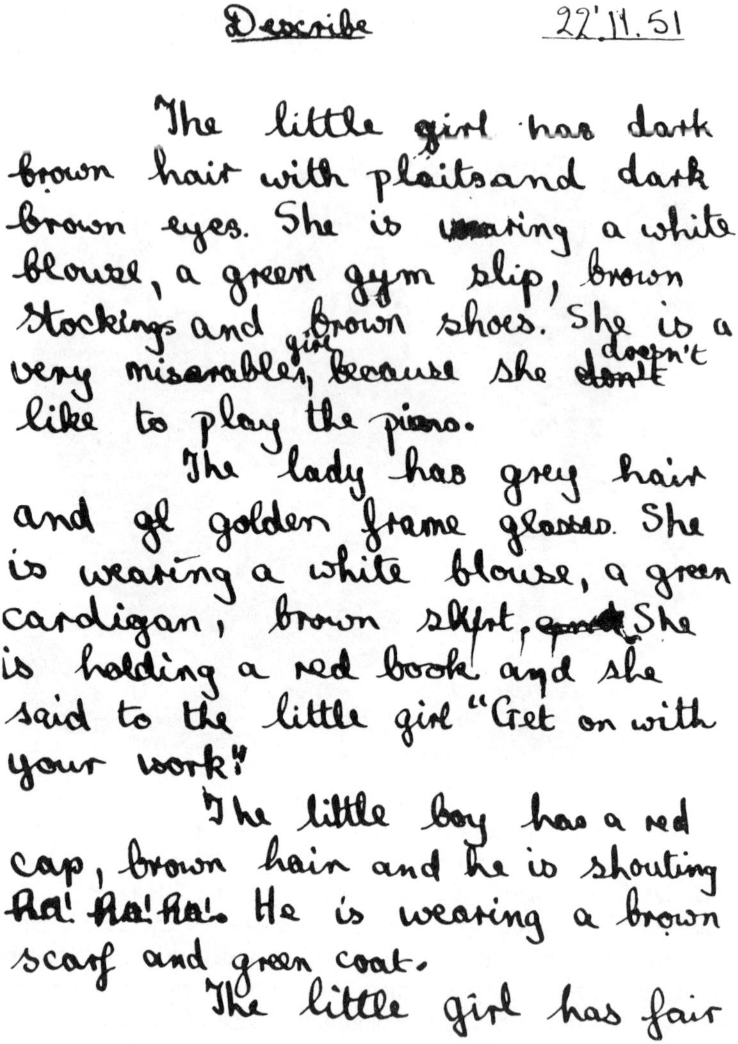

Describe   22'.11.51

The little girl has dark brown hair with plaits and dark brown eyes. She is wearing a white blouse, a green gym slip, brown stockings and brown shoes. She is a very miserable, because she doesn't like to play the piano.

The lady has grey hair and gl golden frame glasses. She is wearing a white blouse, a green cardigan, brown skirt, She is holding a red book and she said to the little girl "Get on with your work."

The little boy has a red cap, brown hair and he is shouting Ha! Ha! Ha! He is wearing a brown scarf and green coat.

The little girl has fair

FIG. 101a (reduced)

The headmaster's comment was, 'A very accurate description.'
The common factors traced in the drawings and handwritings of

these ten deaf children are loneliness, withdrawal, tension, anxiety, lack of security, a sense of frustration and a feeling of guilt. They all have a vertical or reversed angle of writing, which may be partly due to their school copy but which shows that these handicapped children do not feel at their ease when confronted by more fortunate children who are not thwarted as they are. Deaf children avoid mixing with those of normal hearing for their interests differ widely. They cannot get rid of their feeling of inferiority, which is, alas often due to the fact that their own families and even parents make them realise that they are a burden.

This feeling of inadequacy is frequently followed by a releasing outburst of anger, for their emotions are easily upset, and this in turn is followed by a feeling of guilt. Inside their own world deaf children are sociable, although apt to disagree violently. Their inability to hear tends to slow down their rhythm, so that their actions are generally retarded.

The graphological findings in this chapter do not suggest that skill in drawing is correlated with general intelligence as defined by Professor Spearman. Inner conflict, maladjustment and frustrations may impede intellectual achievements and yet may lead to wonderful results in self-expression in other than academic fields.

Deaf children are often intuitive and ingenious. Their inspirations come from spiritual and emotional sources rather than from external experiences. It is revealing to observe how expressive the drawings of deaf children are. These children are often considered backward, but their standard, as revealed in their designs and in their handwritings, should refute the conception of their mental retardation. Each and all can stand alone, their performances comparing well with those of "normal children."

In the following chapter the deaf children will be paired with ten non-handicapped children of the same age-group for purposes of comparison.

CHAPTER TEN

Handwritings and Drawings of "Normal" Children

The ten examples of handwritings and drawings studied in this chapter were produced by children of a County Primary School. The headmaster made a few marginal remarks on the reports such as 'Yes', 'Correct' or 'This is just like him', but where he did not know the pupil well he made no remark at all.

Figures 102 and 103 are the work of identical twins, Ronald and Bobby, aged nine years.

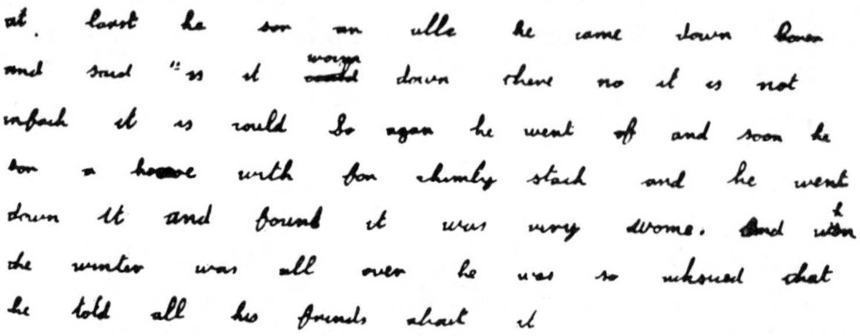

FIG. 102a (reduced)

At a glance one would say that their writings are alike, but analysis shows that Ronald's hand (Fig. 102a) betrays a dulled and blurred mentality. His orthography is quite hopeless: it is almost impossible to decipher his words and their meaning can be guessed only from the context. Ronald's pressure is excessive, an indication that he lives under pressure. He appears to be badly inhibited, to have a weak constitution and to be more truthful or less artful than his twin brother. Ronald's poorer abilities cause him to feel inferior, and this feeling may in its turn be the key to his inadequate achievements.

Ronald's drawing (Fig. 102), however, is rather effective in its simplicity, though showing a melancholic mind. The trees in the winter scenery are bare and stand stark against the dull sky. The black bird is seen in flight, with expanded wings actually in motion. The question that arises is: How can a dull child produce an expressive picture by very simple means? An answer could be found in the contention that Ronald is not backward but frustrated. He would probably do better if he were taught apart from his brother so that he might work without having to suffer odious comparisons.

Bobby, the other twin, is a sensitive, capricious, highly-strung

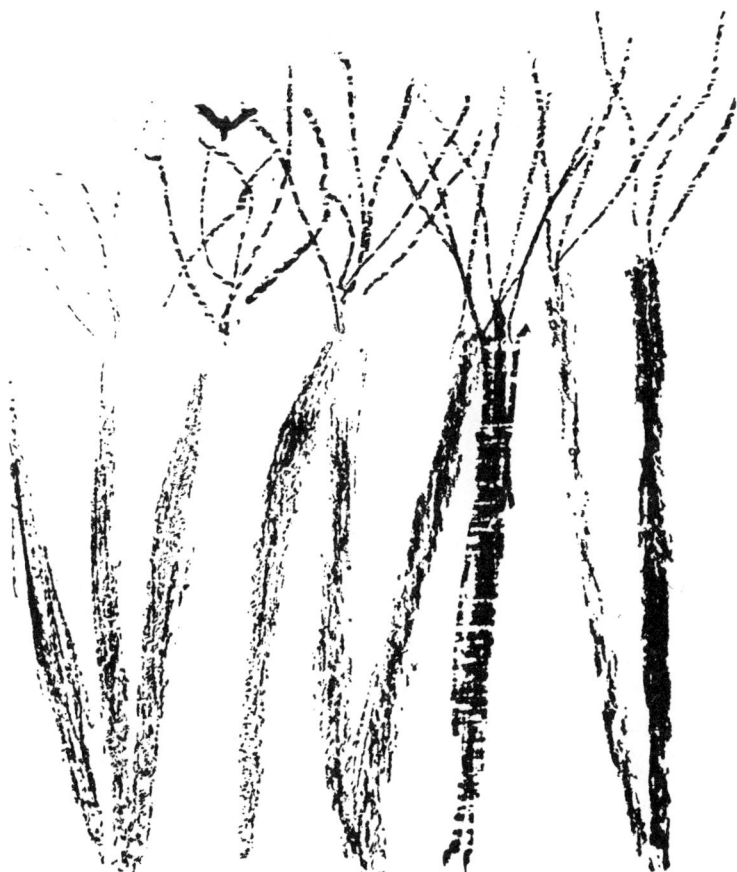

FIG. 102 (reduced)

child who is quick in the uptake. On superficial observation he makes an excellent impression, although he is far from being well-balanced. He likes to appear grand and is a splendid pretender.

He gains favour by means of his sanctimonious behaviour. This is hard on Ronald who really has a more reliable character than Bobby as well as more manual dexterity. Bobby's strong pressure in his handwriting suggests resistance (Fig. 103a). He likes to have

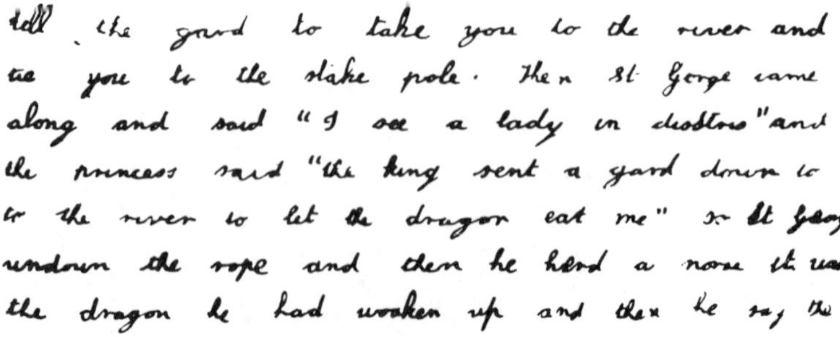

tell the guard to take you to the river and tie you to the stake pole. Then St George came along and said "I see a lady in distress" and the princess said "the king sent a guard down to to the river to let the dragon eat me" so St George undone the rope and then he heard a noise it was the dragon he had woken up and then he say the

FIG. 103a (reduced)

FIG. 103 (reduced)

things all his own way, and he stands independent and aloof.

Bobby's drawing (Fig. 103) shows a childish conception of St. George and the Dragon. The dragon is better drawn than the man. The lines on the animal's body and legs show an infantile interpretation. A child of five might have done equally well.

The headmaster's comment was, 'The suggestion that Bobby and Ronald differ in ability is perfectly true. Bobby is more advanced in all subjects and his personality is brighter, but he is not an offensive child, neither to his brother nor to the class. Ronald is

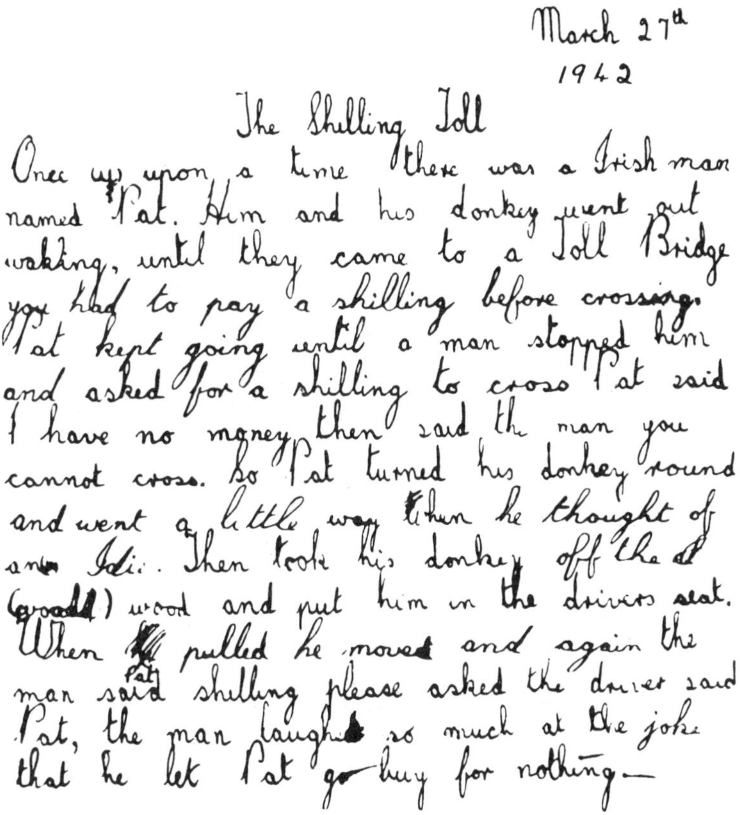

March 27th

1942

The Shilling Toll

Once up upon a time there was a Irish man named Pat. Him and his donkey went out walking, until they came to a Toll Bridge you had to pay a shilling before crossing. Pat kept going until a man stopped him and asked for a shilling to cross Pat said I have no money, then said the man you cannot cross. So Pat turned his donkey round and went a little way then he thought of an Idi. Then took his donkey off the (goodd) wood and put him in the drivers seat. When he pulled he moved and again the man said shilling please asked the driver said Pat, the man laughed so much at the joke that he let Pat go buy for nothing.—

FIG. 104a (reduced)

slow but methodical. He has not got the carefree attitude his brother is endowed with.'

Figure 104a shows the work of Ida who is 10 years old. The writing is all over the place. The slant, the size of the letters, the size ratios and the pressure are all quite irregular and give evidence of Ida's instability.

The frequent corrections as in 'when' (line 9), 'wood' (line 11) and the crossing through seven times of the word 'he' (line 12) indicate destructive impulses while the highly drawn up letters throughout the script are due to the child's ambition. It is in fact likely that the inability to reach her goal may be one of the causes of her state of mind. The girl is not likely to produce positive achievements until she gets help to conquer her difficulties by means of psychotherapy.

FIG. 104 (reduced)

In contrast with her writing is the stiff and rigid expression of her drawing (Fig. 104). There is no movement whatsoever. A stationary cart, a little man sitting in it, a motionless figure by its side, both out of proportion in size, and a donkey which looks like a horse constitute the picture. The drawing is not well put into the available space and artistically it is not worthy of praise. Ida seems to be rather clumsy in her movements. The instability expressed in her handwriting and the rigidity of her drawing, although apparently contradictory, are actually complementary, inasmuch as anxiety and fear cause both her instability and a stagnation due to lack of security.

Figures 105 and 105a show the work of Ernest who is aged 9 years and 6 months.

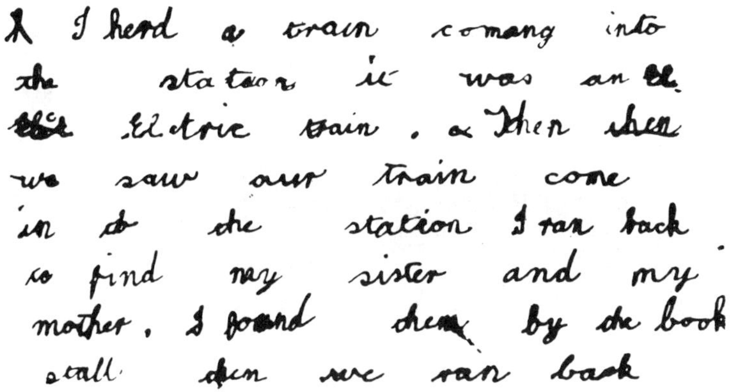

FIG. 105a (reduced)

Ernest is an inhibited boy who tries his best to work conscientiously. His mode of expression, if one takes the text also into consideration, is all one might expect from a boy of his age. The corrections and retracings in his handwriting (Fig. 105a) are unhealthy symptoms and suggest a neurotic disposition, while the strong and irregular pressure points in the same direction. We are dealing with a submissive boy, who, although kind at heart, is not open in character.

His drawing (Fig. 105) is well done and expressive. The station clock, the bookstall, the porter wheeling the luggage-trolley, the station-master and Ernest's brother, can be easily recognized.

The porter moving along with big strides is an interesting achievement.

FIG. 105 (reduced)

The headmaster's comment was, 'Quite a good description.'

Figures 106 and 106a show the work of Charles who is also 9 years 6 months old.

Here we have a very nervy and lonely child who appears to be retarded in development. His spelling and writing are so poor that the words cannot be read but must be surmised. Charles can, however, express himself more clearly in his drawing which is excellent in perspective. The boy seems to be repressed and trying to conform to his circumstances. He is self-centred, finds it difficult to make social contacts and is afraid to speak the truth from fear of punishment. He obviously hates writing (Fig. 106a) and tries to get the burdensome task over as quickly as possible.

The picture (Fig. 106) is quite another matter. It is rather

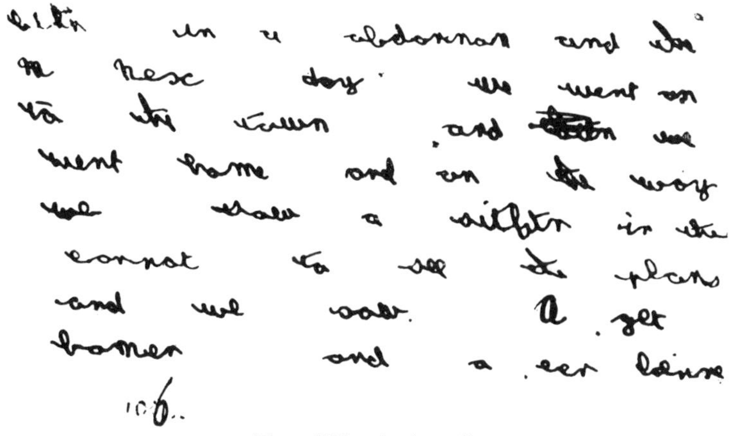

FIG. 106a (reduced)

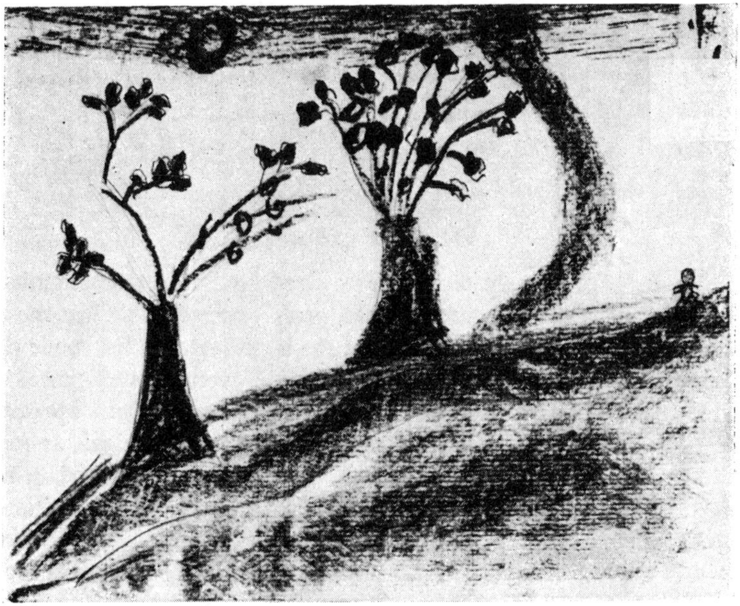

FIG. 106 (reduced)

original, showing productive ability and a good sense of observation. The sunshine spreads over the trees which are well executed in perspective, the road is winding and the lawns each side of the path are expressive. This drawing, compared with Charles's unsatisfactory achievements in other school subjects, is promising. His writing and his drawing are in no way identical in value. In drawing the boy can express his thoughts, in ordinary lessons he is rather hopeless.

The headmaster's remark was, 'This is Charles exactly.'

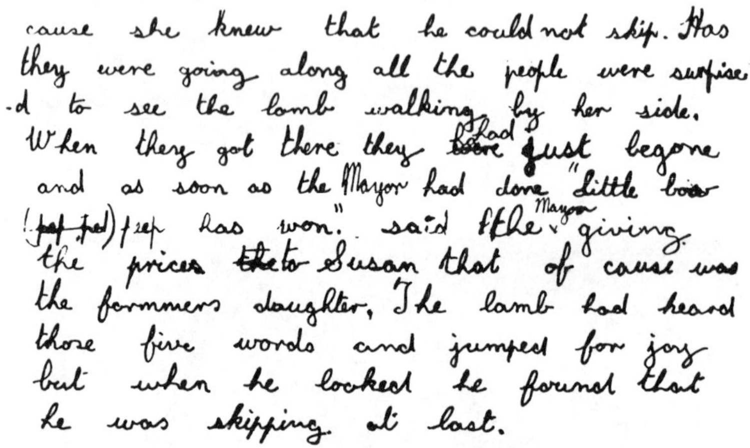

cause she knew that he could not skip. Has
they were going along all the people were surprise
-d to see the lamb walking by her side.
When they got there they had just begone
and as soon as the Mayor had done "little boo
(pef pef) pep has won." said ffhe Mayor giving
the prices thheto Susan that of cause was
the formmers daughter, The lamb had heard
those five words and jumped for joy
but when he looked he found that
he was skipping at last.

FIG. 107a (reduced)

Figure 107 shows the work of Margaret, aged 10 years 9 months.

Margaret is a kind girl and she gives expression to her most compelling emotions. In many ways she is primitive in her mode of expression, but all the same she has a good average intelligence.

Margaret's letter-formation is partly frayed and the girl appears to be uncertain of herself. Her capital M's are emphasized, as for example in 'Mayor.' This suggests a certain measure of self-aggrandisement, her Christian name beginning with M. The initials are laboured and constrained indicating the peculiarity of her individuality. She is at war with orthography and spells more or less phonetically. In line 1, she adds an h to 'as', which is significant of her background. She relates her story in a childish manner, but shows at the same time some creative ability, which we find repeated in her fairly full loops. The words 'has' and 'the', for example, in line 6 show an exaggerated h loop, and others are discernible throughout the script.

FIG. 107 (normal size)

Her drawing is charming. A delightful, graceful movement is visible. Margaret and Booboo are walking together, Margaret carrying a shepherdess's staff in her left hand and the lamb on the lead. The bow on the lamb's neck and those in Margaret's hair and on the staff give evidence of her love of details which are meticulously attended to. The words written in capital script are neatly done too.

Figure 108a shows the work of Arthur, aged 10 years 9 months.

The spelling and letter-formation are those of a backward child. The shapes are hopeless as if produced by a boy of seven and suggest that Arthur has a low I.Q. Many retracements and corrections do not improve the legibility of a script that is indistinct. The mangled letters, shaky strokes and filled-up loops are all symptoms pointing in one direction and leading to the conclusion that Arthur is a psychopathic case. His communication is senseless and inane, partly because of the faulty spelling and partly because of the boy's

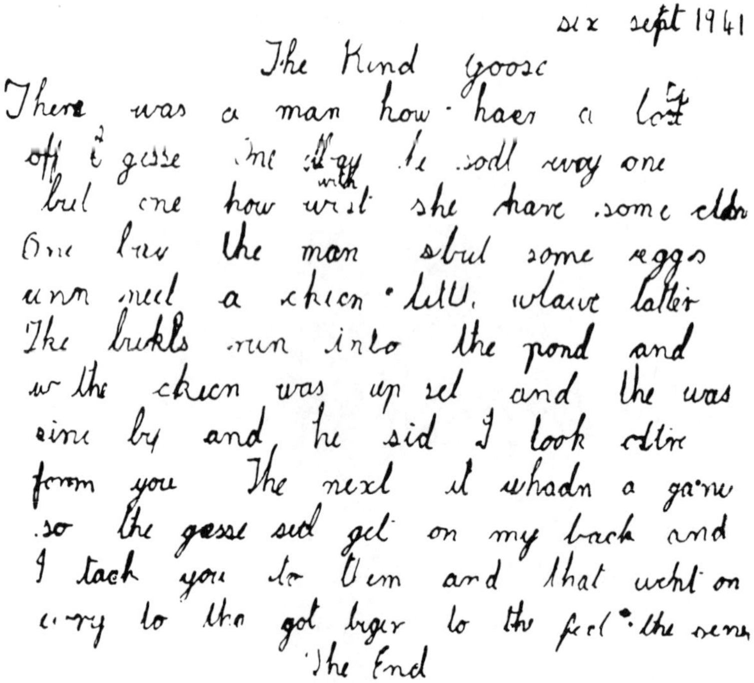

six sept 1941

The Kind Goose

There was a man how haes a lot
off e goose one day he sold evay one
but one how wist she have some chin
One day the man stud some eggs
unn nul a chicn lill. wlave later
The bukls run into the pond and
w the chicn was up sel and the was
sine by and he sid I look dtn
form you The next it whadn a gane
so the gosse sed get on my back and
I tack you to Uem and that ucht on
e ry to tho got bigr to th feel the sens
The End

FIG. 108a (reduced)

lack of dexterity. His untruthfulness must be considered part and parcel of his condition.

When comparing his handwriting with his drawing (Fig. 108) we come to a different conclusion about Arthur. The hen, the goose and the chickens are well set into the space and there is even a trace of perspective discernible. The border too is quite artistically conceived. At any rate the boy can express himself much more clearly in his drawing than in his handwriting. This leads to the inference that Arthur is not so much of low intelligence as of high excitability.

Figures 109 and 109a show the work of Molly, aged 11 years 8 months.

Molly is a clever, versatile, ambitious and sensitive girl who likes to show off for the sake of being admired. In spite of her pale handwriting (Fig. 109a) which might suggest that she is physically weak,

162

FIG. 108 (reduced)

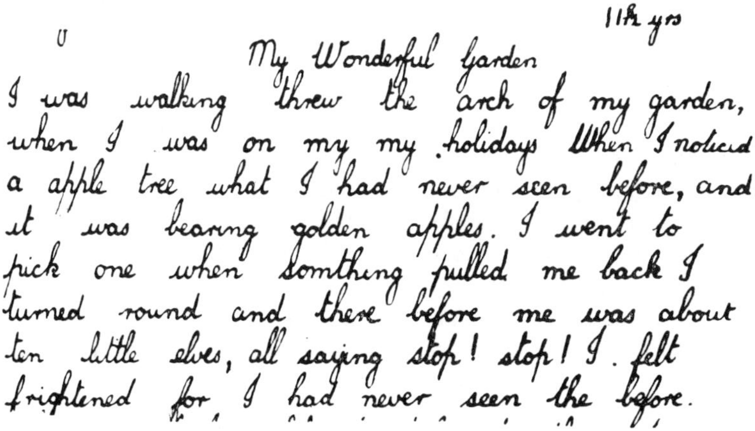

11½ yrs

My Wonderful Garden

I was walking threw the arch of my garden,
when I was on my my holidays When I noticed
a apple tree what I had never seen before, and
it was bearing golden apples. I went to
pick one when somthing pulled me back I
turned round and there before me was about
ten little elves, all saying stop! stop! I felt
frightened for I had never seen the before.

FIG. 109a (reduced)

much vitality is expended on strong pressure. Her 'I's' are peculiarly constrained, stiff and pointed, a symptom of aggression against herself, but no other signs of outbreaks of temper can be seen in her writing. Some of the strokes show plasticity of mind and this evidence is repeated in her drawings. She is, however, more painstaking than gifted.

FIG. 109 (reduced)

Her drawing (Fig. 109) is clever and expressive. The garden path, the arch overgrown with roses, the golden apples on the tree, the flowers surrounding the apple tree are all well carried out. Her self-portrait is not too flattering, and the figure under the arch is as stiff and unyielding as her 'I's'. There is an expression of fear on her face which could be identified with the constrained ego shown in her handwriting.

The headmaster's comment was, 'She looks anaemic but her health is good and she is full of vitality. She is clever and versatile.'

Figure 110 shows the work of Teddy, aged 10 years 9 months.

The drawing is the attempt of an artist in the making and would do justice to a much older and more mature child. The horse is

FIG. 110 (reduced)

frisky, roaming about a meadow which is surrounded by a wooden fence. The muscles of the horse are contracted and the expression on its face is sophisticated and very intelligent, in fact almost alive.

It is strange to observe that Teddy's handwriting (Fig. 110a) bears no relation to his excellent drawing. It is all in a tangle and far from praiseworthy. That the boy is troubled by an inferiority complex is evidenced by the tiny writing used for the word 'Tom' (line 3). In fact all his writing is small and produced slowly. The text can only be guessed for it is illegible. This pitifully poor attempt at conveying his thoughts in writing is in marked contrast with his accomplished drawing. A boy who can draw so well cannot, one would suppose, be of inferior intelligence, and yet the writing indicates a low I.Q. Not shown is a tiny pencil sketch on the same page as the writing. It is most artistically drawn and yet the boy does not know how to spell 'horse.' This is truly puzzling. Might there be a strong antipathy to the teachers, a resistance to the representatives of authority? This would impede Teddy's potentialities. The filled-up loops in the 'f' of the word 'farmer' (line 1), the neglected loops in almost all the 'h's' and in some of the 'l's' suggest a dreamy mentality, as if the boy could not think clearly or

165

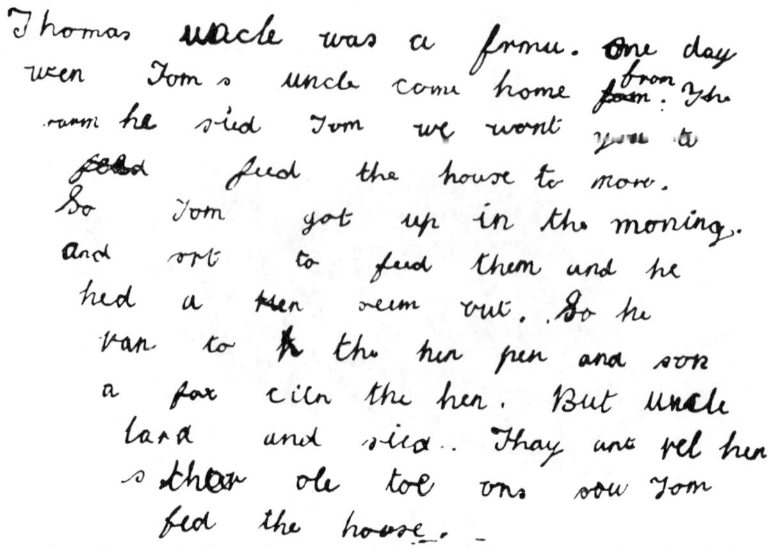

FIG. 110a (reduced)

express his thoughts lucidly. Teddy's drawing and his handwriting cannot be brought into harmony however one may try. Perhaps his teacher might be able to throw some light on this problem.

The headmaster's comment was, 'He is in the 'C' stream. Loves to draw and will do so all day.'

Figures 111 and 111a show the work of Sonia, aged 11 years 5 months.

The text, a pretty little fairy tale about the relationship between a mother and child is the outcome of a very sensitive and kind nature. This is borne out by the neat and conscientious execution of Sonia's handwriting (Fig. 111a). Without any doubt this child has congenial home conditions. She seems also to be musical, or at least to take an interest in music, for some of her letter-formations look like musical symbols e.g. the capital S in 'Susan' (line 1), 'She' (line 8).

Sonia is advanced and intelligent, but we observe many resting points in her handwriting. These points denote that her hand rested on the paper while she paused to consider how to formulate her story, and they indicate a lack of spontaneity and a slow rhythm. In spite of a good parent-child relationship Sonia is inhibited and therefore has no ease in expressing herself. Her 'I' (line 10) also gives the impression of a constrained personality. She is extremely ambitious and her competitive urge causes some repressions. The writing in general is rather pale, which suggests that Sonia's physical

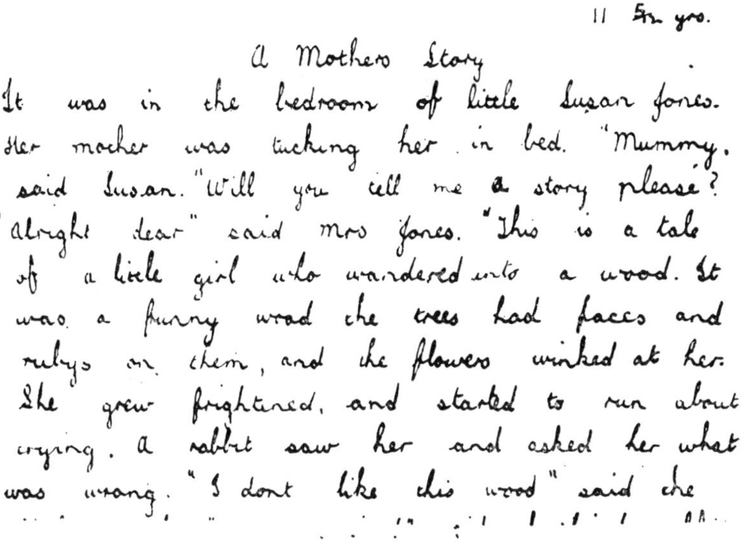

11 &n. yrs.

A Mother's Story

It was in the bedroom of little Susan Jones. Her mother was tucking her in bed. "Mummy," said Susan. "Will you tell me a story please?" "Alright dear" said Mrs Jones. "This is a tale of a little girl who wandered into a wood. It was a funny wood the trees had faces and eyes on them, and the flowers winked at her. She grew frightened, and started to run about crying. A rabbit saw her and asked her what was wrong. "I dont like this wood" said the

FIG. 111a (reduced)

health is not robust. The short lower projections (the loops in f, g, p and y) also indicate a weak central nervous system. Sonia is a very likeable girl and usually does everything expected of her irrespective of the trouble it may cause her. She is not socially minded and prefers to keep detached: she thus has some difficulty in making contacts.

In considering Sonia's drawing we find a similar subject—glimpses of home conditions—to those in Figures 97 and 98 of the deaf children, Lena and Laura. The deaf children's productions are, however, much bolder than Sonia's. This may be due in part to the size of the paper which was given to them. Sonia's drawing is delicate and

"Will you tell me a story mummy"?

"It was a lovely little room with pink curtains a fireplace Saba table and everything"

FIG. 111 (reduced)

denotes a gift of detailed observation. She lies in bed, her mother sitting by her side telling her a story. This is very realistically expressed, even to the pattern on the wallpaper and the embroidered butterfly on her pillowslip. The room in which the little rabbit lives is just delightful. The pink curtains at the window, the portrait on the wall (one of the little rabbit family), the fireplace with its neatly arranged chimney-piece ornamented with a clock and with vases filled with flowers, the carpet, the table, the chair and the couch prove that Sonia comes from a well-ordered home. The delicacy of the colouring and the cheerful atmosphere of the place are most refreshing, but at the same time the detail gives evidence that Sonia was brought up in a somewhat too conventional setting which has impeded her natural rhythm. This can also be seen in her handwriting.

The immobility and the general stiffness of the design, as well as that of the handwriting, suggest a puritanical upbringing. The mother spreads an atmosphere of calm and repose, but at the same time sets too high a standard for the child, thus causing frustrations and inhibitions.

To the statements that Sonia has a very sensitive and kind nature and that she is musical, the headmaster says, 'Correct' in the margin. To the observation that Sonia is a likeable girl who does everything that is expected of her, he puts 'Yes.'

In this group, as in that of the deaf children, some drawings e.g. Figures 105, 106 and 110 suggest that a gift for drawing does not necessarily betoken general intelligence. In some instances it appears that inner conflict, maladjustment, a feeling of inferiority, inhibitions and frustrations may impede the faculty of expressing the pupil's intelligence in writing and yet may lead to amazing skill in drawing. In the material examined here it is evident that drawing skill is, at any rate, not closely correlated with intelligence but that remarkable drawings are sometimes coupled with poor scholarship. Only research on a much wider scale could decide whether this is a general finding.

Drawing skill appears accompanied by writing of two kinds however. A quite good picture may be found with refined neat letter-forms written with care and with light pressure as in Figures 109a and 111a. But it may be accompanied by awkward, careless and untidy writing as in Figures 105a, 106, 107a and 110a where the drawings, contrary to expectations aroused by the poor writing, show signs of clever draughtsmanship.

In comparing the work of deaf and normal children we should give weight to the fact that deaf children have considerable individual attention, for the teachers take a special interest in their charges and have had a very careful training for the purpose of helping the deaf. These teachers take only small groups and are not bound by fixed standards. In the case of Primary Council Schools, on the other hand, it is not expedient to apply an individual approach and therefore imagination and intuition cannot be fostered.

CONCLUSION

Graphology has been far too long in the embryo stage of its development and therefore only a few results of scientific research are so far available. We recognize, however, a definite and encouraging advance when we read old manuals of graphology and realize how much has been achieved in the last thirty years. The very fact that sign-reading is obsolete today, and that only a complex of signs, all leading the graphologist to the same conclusion, can be valid when diagnosing the character of a penman, is a welcome step in the right direction.

Saudek in his Tables of Speed has given us leading principles for the assessment of handwritings, but much research remains to be done. The author would consider her efforts in writing this book a success if it would stimulate some of her colleagues to set out on extensive research. For example all psychological tests ought to be followed up by graphological tests and research. This would give graphology a higher standing than it now has, and at the same time give the lie to the popular idea that it is merely some kind of black magic or no better than tea-leaf reading.

Graphology, as pointed out in the Introduction, has its limitations, but many of its shortcomings will disappear in the light of research. It can undoubtedly become a perfect tool in the hands of the initiated, helping them in the work of solving the difficult human problems that come within the scope of psychology.

In this book the author has dealt principally with human problems which by their very nature create disturbing reading. This should not however lead the reader to conclude that graphology is a gloomy profession. Whenever we are confronted with healthy and noble character-structures ample exhilaration and inspiration compensate the graphologist for his labours.

Accuracy:
Slow and natural handwriting
Good general spacing
Regular pressure
Certainty of aim
Careful execution of letter formation
Regularity
Simplifications
Adhering to school-copy
Increased size-ratios

Aesthetic Criticism:
Simplifications
Beautiful and original forms
Good inner and outer spacing
Right margin
Originality of connections
No strong pressure
Speed and naturalness are not essential
Psychological Interpretation: love of beauty, refinement, artistic taste, when combined with a high standard originality or even creative power.

Affection:
Rounded forms
Primary wide and secondary wide
No curtailed characters
Slanting hand
Some variability

Ambition:
Complex of Vanity
Complex of Inhibitions
Emphasis of size-ratio
Complex of Mental Activity
Fairly high standard

Amiability:
Good outer spacing
Wide script
Amplifications
Garlands
Speed
Slant

Avarice:
Slow hand
No margins
Lines and words are close together
Narrow script
Angular style
Lack of rounded forms
Disconnected hand
Small script
Symptoms of accuracy
Tendency to the left

Audacity: (*Blind Courage*)
The same symptoms as in Courage
Slanting writing
Initial underemphasis
Bad spacing
Exaggerated signature
Variability

Calculating: (*harsh and callous*)
Rigid angularity
Narrowness
Covering strokes
Final emphasis
Final adjustments
Tendency to the left
Initial adjustments

Capable Organiser:
Quick tempo
Good spacing

Certain irregularity is permissible, but should be outbalanced by symptoms of Harmony
Originality of connections and letter formation
Certain simplifications
Complex of Energy
Some symptoms of Diplomacy
Some symptoms of Self-control
No excessive slant
Natural hand

Capriciousness:
Irregular and indistinct spacing
Irregular writing-angle
Irregular size and size-ratios
Wide and narrow writing
Variability of connections
Sometimes sudden angles
Variability of shapes
Thready connections
Change of the grip of the pen
Final emphasis
Final adjustments

Concealment:
Arcades
Slow hand
Neglected size-ratios
Narrowness (covering strokes)
Reversed style of writing
Pseudo-garlands
Unnaturalness
Decreased left margin
Thready connections
Strong tendency to the left
Embellishments

Control of Egoism:
Tendency to the right in a natural hand
Garland style
Rounded forms

No arcades
Slanting hand
Vertical style when according to school-copy
Wide script
Slight initial emphasis
Simplified forms
No marked final emphasis
Only slight irregularity or variability

Convention:
Normal average National alphabet
Unnatural writing
Circumstantial initial emphasis
Sometimes indications of Hypocrisy

Conscientiousness:
Careful shaping of characters with originality
Adaptability of connections
Certainty of aim
Regularity without uniformity
Some variations in size, writing-angle and width

Courage:
Quick tempo
Spontaneity
Width
Pressure
Tendency to angularity
No small script
If combined with symptoms of Intelligence, Criticism or Wisdom, it is the determination of a person who knows his own mind

Cowardice:
Complex of Timidity
Complex of Ostentation
Complex of Vanity

173

Criticism:
  Simplifications
  Good spacing
  Certain originality of connections and characters
  Certain irregularity, but must be outbalanced by some symptoms of Harmony
  Certain amount of consistency
  Symptoms of regularity
  No emphasised size-ratios
  No large script
  Neither extreme speed nor slowness
  Natural hand
  Psychological Interpretation: sense of proportion, matter of fact sense, objectivity and wit.

Diligence:
  Quick hand
  Regular pressure
  No marked variability
  Carefully shaped characters
  Careful placing of i-dots

Diplomacy:
  Indistinct connections
  Arcades
  Characters which are illegible
  Pseudo-garlands
  Irregularity
  No uniformity
  Decreased size-ratios
  Intellectual standard
  Fairly good spacing
  Certain originality of connections

Disguise:
  Reversed style of writing
  Tendency to the left
  Occasional arcades

  Initial emphasis or under-emphasis
  Unnaturalness

Distrust:
  Restricted writing tempo
  Narrow script
  Arcades, sometimes mixed with angular connections
  No large script
  No initial emphasis
  Final adjustments
  Prolonged final strokes to fill the space between words

Dogmatism:
  Complex of Idealism
  Lack of Intellectual Criticism
  Lack of Aesthetic Criticism

Domineering:
  Amplifications
  Prolonged t-bars with final adjustments
  Strong pressure
  Angular style
  Final adjustments
  Final emphasis
  Initial adjustments (not essential)

Easy-going:
  Unfinished characters
  Rounded forms
  Slow tempo
  Secondary width
  Variability
  Neither purely angular nor arcade style of connections
  Either garlands, indistinct or even thready connections

Egoism:
  Strong tendency to the left
  Reversed angle of writing
  Initial emphasis by enlargement

Ornamentation and a moody
originality of conspicuous
letters
Slight final emphasis
Angular style
Narrowness
Lack of harmony

Empathy:
Sensitiveness
Quick judgment and observation
Self-criticism
Garlands

Energy:
Quick hand
Normal pressure
Rising lines
Certain irregularity is possible
but must be outbalanced by
some symptoms of discipline (good spacing, certainty of aim, regularity of
pressure)
No thready connections
Increased left margin

Exhaustion from Sexual Causes:
Pasty writing
Slow writing
Lack of pressure
Broken or curved lower projections
Covering strokes
Final adjustments
Resting points
Sinking lines
Broken strokes
Unfinished characters

Expediency:
Pseudo-garlands
Writing tempo speeded up by
routine
Lack of distinctness in
characters

Neglected size-ratios
Variability or lability
Mannerism in width
Regular change of primary
wide and secondary narrow
writing

Feminine Attitude:
Lack of pressure
Slow hand
Pasty writing
Variability or lability
Refined rounded forms
Reduced size-ratios (in
female as well as male)

Generosity:
Quick hand
Large script
Variety of style
Good inner spacing
Width
Garlands
Enrichments

Harmony:
Slightly reduced size-ratios
Consistency in size-ratios
(upper and lower projections are not identical in
size but are well proportioned)
Excellent balanced spacing
Natural hand
No marked regularity
No marked uniformity

Haphazardness: (*adventurer*)
Disconnected characters
Illegibility
Uncertainty of aim
Irregularity of all features
(size, size-ratios, width,
slant)
Amplifications

Hypocrisy:
Retarded tempo
Initial emphasis or under-
emphasis
Degenerated 'I's'
Signature smaller than the
preceding text
Covering strokes
Pseudo-garlands
Indistinct letter formation

Hysteria:
Type A
Enrichments
Lability
Irregularity of all features
Bad inner and outer spacing
Suddenly swelling pressure
Sudden break in downstrokes
Some symptoms of the Men-
dacity Complex
Type B
Copperplate style and careful
and deliberate shaping of
letters
Stylish hand
Reversed style of writing
Unnaturalness
Marked initial emphasis
Some symptoms of the Men-
dacity Complex

Idealism:
Large script
Natural script
Highly placed diacritics
Emphasis of the upper projec-
tions
Fairly high standard
Refined shaping of characters
No strong pressure

Imagination:
Amplified ornamental hand
Large script

Variability
Positive or negative originality
Curved forms
If the ornamentation and
originality are exaggerated
so ostentatiously as to
appear bizarre, and if the
spacing is bad, we are dealing with fantasy formations.

Impatience:
Broken strokes
Tremor
Atactic strokes
Sinking lines
Covering strokes but also
width
Increasing left margin

*Impatience from Nervous
Causes*:
Great variability of most
features
Increasing left margin
Disconnections within the
words
Overconnections with other
words
Final pressure
Thready connections

Indolence:
Slow hand
Omission of parts of letters
Primary wide and secondary
wide writing
Reduced size-ratios
Lack of vertical readjustment
Lack of pressure
Illegibility
Bad spacing
Untidiness
Garlands in a slow hand or
inconsistent connections

Inferiority:
  Hesitating tempo
  Initial underemphasis
  Small script
  Tendency to sinking lines
  Variability of at least two features
  No conspicuous but plainly legible signature
  Simplifications
  Narrowness
  Corrections
  Inhibitions
  In prominent cases trembling strokes
  Thready connections
  Lack of pressure
  Wavy lines

Inhibitions:
  Many contradictions (inconsistencies)
  Irregularity
  Narrowness
  Retardation of the script with occasional tendency to speed

Inner Conflict:
  Variability of all elements
  Indistinct connections
  Bad inner spacing
  Irregular general spacing
  Inconsistencies of initial emphasis and underemphasis
  Sudden angularity

Intellectuality:
  Quick hand
  Simplifications
  Aesthetic formation of characters
  Good spacing

  Clever connections
  Originality
  Modest signature
  When coupled with vanity the same but in addition: —
  Initial ornamentation
  Emphasized signature
  Underlining of certain words to give emphasis
  Genuine originality but ostentatiously shown: —
  Final emphasis
  Reduced tempo
  Wasting of writing surface at the head of paper (large upper margin)

Intellectual Balance:
  Good spacing
  Quick hand
  Balanced size-ratios
  Simplified forms
  Legibility

Intellectual Criticism:
  Neither extreme speed nor extreme slowness
  Simplifications
  Good spacing
  No large script
  Certain originality of connections

Intuition:
  Symptoms of sensitivity
  Slight pressure
  Variability
  No laborious adjustments
  Not too simplified but somewhat amplified script
  Quick hand
  Superior intellect
  Originality of connections and letter formations

Irritability:
Marked variability of all elements
Lability
Bad spacing
Frequent inconsistencies
Strong irregular pressure
Sudden angularity
Tendency to the left
Contradictory signs of speed
Partly written quickly, partly slowly

Jealousy:
Sensitiveness and Selfishness combined

Lability:
Lack of pressure or slight pressure
Indistinct or thready connections
Variability of most symptoms: size, size-ratio, slant, width, pressure
Either extreme slant or reversed angle

Lack of Adaptability:
Bad spacing
Final adjustments
Angularity
Final enlargements
Narrowness
Disconnected style
Variability
Either exaggerated simplifications impairing legibility or
Exaggerated simplifications not doing so
Large script

Lack of Balance:
Irregularity of writing-angle
Uncertainty of aim
Bad spacing

Lack of Inhibitions:
Wide script
Increased left margin
Indistinct connections
Lateral holding of the pen
Variability
Lack of pressure.
Neglected letter forms

Lack of Self-criticism:
Amplifications
Complicated adjustments
Bad spacing
Negative originality
Lack of consistency
Unnaturalness
Large script
Emphasized size-ratio
Initial underemphasis
Reduced legibility
Thready connections

Lack of Self-reliance:
Hesitating tempo
Initial underemphasis
Lack of pressure
Rounded or distinct forms of connections
Variability
Bad spacing
Frequent errors in writing
Symptoms of Irritability
No originality
A pedantic hand not deviating from school-copy

Lack of Self-control:
Irregular writing-angle
Variability of style
Slanting hand
Careless execution particularly in inconspicuous parts
Primarily wide and secondarily wide writing
Uncertainty of aim
Bad spacing

Laziness:
Continuity in a slow hand
Frequent interruptions with immediate adjustments
Uncertainty of aim
Lack of readjustment of the paper
The end of the page is crowded
Neglect of size-ratios
Neglect of shaping of characters to illegibility
Garlands or inconsistent connections
Lack of pressure
Resting points
Initial or final adjustments

Love of Comfort:
Slow hand
Lack of adjustment of the forearm towards the end of the line
Increased slant and increased connections
Unfinished characters
Decreased size towards the end of every word
Pseudo-garland style
Occasionally increased size-ratios

Masculine Attitude:
Pressure
Activity
Firmness
Simplifications
Final adjustments
Symptoms of Self-confidence

Materialism:
Coarse shape of characters
Heavy pressure
Bad spacing
Pastiness

Emphasis of lower projections
Untidy hand
Tendency to the left
Angular style

Mendacity:
Slow handwriting
Unnatural hand
Lability
Touching up and corrections which do not improve the shape nor legibility of the script
Some letters show neglected size-ratios so that different letters than were intended are produced
Covering strokes
Blobs or punctuated handwriting
Characters written with three or four strokes of the pen
Omission of important parts of characters
Marked initial emphasis
The letters, a, o, d, g, q, are open at the base thus forming arcades (half-ovals turning to the left)
Thready connections

Mental Activity:
Several signs of speed
Variability (size, size-ratios, width)
Change of the grip of the pen
Variability in shaping of characters
Certain originality of characters
Psychological Interpretation:
impressionability, imagination, original ideas, sensitiveness, moodiness, lack of balance, inner contradictions

Modesty: (*lack of vanity*)
Natural hand
Initial underemphasis
Final emphasis
Inconspicuous c h a r a c t e r s
neglected in a slow hand
Sometimes a reversed angle of
writing

Obstinacy:
Final emphasis
Final adjustments
Angular style
Strong pressure
Bad spacing
Certain initial emphasis

Opportunistic Adaptability:
Variable connections
Width
Either lack of pressure or
lateral holding of the pen
Reduced size-ratios
No ostentation
Mature and easy formations
of characters
No final adjustments
No angularity

Optimism:
Quick hand
Rising lines
Wide script
No emphasis of size-ratios
Good spacing
Certain irregularity
No great consistency
Large script
If simplifications do occur
they must be outbalanced
b y originally s h a p e d
characters

Ostentation:
Large and original shaping of
characters

Unnatural and slow hand
Initial emphasis and initial
adjustments
Amplifications
Ornamentation
Flourishes
Tendency to the left
Reversed angle of writing

Passion:
Several symptoms of Speed
Slanting hand
Pressure not regular
Large script
Some variability
Pastiness
Various symptoms of Inhibi-
tions (sudden angles, sud-
den pressure, narrowness)

Parsimony:
Restricted tempo
No margins
Narrow script
Lines and words close
together
Small script
Simplified script
Symptoms of pedantry
Some tendency to the left

Persistence:
Careful execution
Certainty of aim
Final adjustments
Regularity of conspicuous and
inconspicuous parts of the
script
Angular style
Initial emphasis

Pessimism:
Lack of energy
Lack of balance

Pretended idealism:
The same as Idealism but an
unnatural hand

*Quick Judgment and
Observation*:
Several signs of Speed
Simplifications not impairing
legibility
Natural originality in incon-
spicuous characters
S k i l f u l and appropriate
connections adapted to the
next character
Good horizontal and vertical
spacing
Not very large script
Variability rather than uni-
formity
Diacritics not very high above
the letters

Sadism:
Sensuality
Angularity
Final adjustments
Sudden pressure
Sharply pointed end strokes

Scepticism:
Marked self-criticism
Variability or lability
Lack of balance
Tendency to the left
Sinking lines

Schemer: (*mischief-maker*)
Slow hand
Lack of spontaneity
Narrowness
Angular forms
Several indications of
Diplomacy
Egoism

Self-Assertion:
Vanity
Some inhibitions
Emphasis of size-ratios
Not a very high standard
Good general spacing
Unnatural hand
Initial emphasis
Initial adjustments
Final emphasis
Final adjustments
Enrichments
Amplifications
Tendency to the left
Marked inconsistency
Ostentatious initials and in-
distinct thready connections
are a symptom of the
Delusion of Grandeur
(Megalomania)

Self-Confidence:
Restricted or quick tempo
Some initial emphasis (not
exaggerated)
Naturalness
No inconsistency
No small script
Regular pressure
Firm hand

Self-Control:
Regularity of the writing-
angle
Certainty of aim
Reversed angle of writing
with narrowness
Careful execution particularly
in inconspicuous parts
Uniformity of style
Regular change of primary
narrowness and secondary
width

181

Self-Indulgence:
General looseness
Pastiness
Slant
Variability
Neglected characters
Omitted i-dots
Bad spacing
Slowness
Width

Sense of Reality:
Simplifications
Natural hand
Long lower projections
Good inner spacing
Harmony in all features
Adaptability and originality in connections
No large script
Diacritics not high above the stem

Sensitiveness:
Rounded forms
Variability of all symptoms (size, size - ratios, slant, width, pressure)
Loosely guided pen
Slant
Slight pressure
Refined letter formation

Sensuality:
Pasty writing
Extreme slant
Long lower projections
Loosely guided pen
Sudden irregular pressure
Lack of pressure (in a female hand)
Strong pressure (in a male hand)
Curtailed letters in a slow hand

Garlands or thready connections
Lability

Sentiment: (*emotion*)
Variability
Large natural script
Slanting hand
Impaired spacing
Round letter formations
Amplifications
Sometimes angular style

Sentimentality:
Indistinct connections
Slight pressure
Variability or lability
Some symptoms of Idealism
Embellishments
Tendency to the left
Tempo not very quick

Sincerity:
Quick and natural hand
Distinct connections
No arcades
Not narrow
Certain amount of regularity
Simplifications
No strong tendency to the left
No emphasized adjustments
The better the spacing the greater the sincerity

Spontaneity:
Quick and natural hand
No initial or final adjustments

Superficiality:
Decreased size-ratios
Middle letters equal to small letters
Exaggerated neglect of characters in a quick hand
Omitted parts of letters and omitted i-dots

Width
Lability
Lack of pressure
Wavy lines
Neglected spacing

Talkativeness:
Width
Secondary width
Bad spacing
Tempo speeded up
Letter form lacks distinction
Pseudo-garlands

Timidity:
Hesitating writing tempo
Lack of pressure
Indistinct connections
Variability or lability
Initial underemphasis
Narrowness
Trembling strokes

Tolerance: (*patience*)
Harmony and regularity of most elements
Simplifications or at least no exaggerated amplifications
Moderate size-ratios including initials
Moderate size
Garland style
Quick tempo not essential—a slower person might prove more patient

Truthfulness:
Quick tempo
Tendency to the right
Garland style
Width
Good spacing
Distinct characters
Well-proportioned size-ratios
No superfluous enrichments
No exaggerated initial or final adjustments

Tyranny:
Large script
Angular style
Reversed angle of writing
No slant
Narrow script
Strong pressure
Initial emphasis
Final emphasis
Extended and high t-bars
Final adjustments
Initial adjustments (not essential)

Vanity: (*self-complacency*)
Good general spacing
Unnatural hand
Initial emphasis
Initial adjustments
Final adjustments
Enrichments
Amplifications
Extreme inconsistency of the script: in fact an emphasized contradiction between ostentatious initials and indistinct threadlike connections is a symptom of pathological v a n i t y (megalomania)

Vitality:
Quick hand
Strong pressure
Large script
Final emphasis
Variety
Change of the grip of the pen
Originality of characters

Wisdom:
Complex of Aesthetic Criticism
Complex of Quick Judgment and Observation
Complex of Criticism

INDEX OF COMPLEXES